DIADIDOMI

DIADIDOMI

THE PNEUMA LIFE PROJECT

KIRK ANTHONY FORD

INTRODUCTION

In the silence of a sanctuary, at the tender age of nine, I heard the unmistakable voice of God—a reverberation that set my life's compass toward the enigmatic intersection of faith and economics. Increasing in wisdom and stature with the rigor of an Air Force veteran and the precision of a summa cum laude scholar, I delved into the depths of ancient text and modern metrics, my soul ignited by the quest for divine understanding. With careful steps leading to the founding of a spiritual college—I saw clarity in the Greek 'Diadidomi'. Have we, in our ceaseless pursuit of wealth, overlooked the profound simplicity of Acts 4:35, a blueprint for eradicating poverty etched in the very miracles of Christ? What if the answer to the world's most daunting crisis lies hidden within the fragments of scripture we recite but seldom grasp? Could Jesus, in His divine economy, have imparted wisdom so transformative that it could upend the pillars of modern macroeconomics? As you venture into 'DIADIDOMI', you are invited to challenge the status quo, to unravel the celestial principles that might just hold the key to humanity's gravest dilemmas. But be forewarned: the truths within are as unsettling as they are liberating. Dare you to step beyond the veil of materialism to witness the miracle of divine distribution? Can the echoes of ancient wisdom truly resonate within today's world, offering not just hope, but tangible salvation from the throes of poverty and death? In the next pages lies an odyssey of discovery—a pathway that could lead to the very heart of human fulfillment.

Now, as you stand on the precipice of this work, I invite you to join me in a consortium of enlightenment. Have you ever pondered the root of poverty, the seemingly insatiable void that swallows up prosperity and leaves in its wake a trail of suffering and despair? Have you considered that the answer to this age-old quandary may have been whispered by Jesus Himself, a secret unveiled in the miracle of the loaves and fishes as chronicled in St. John 6:11?

'DIADIDOMI', the act of distribution, was demonstrated by Christ in a manner so miraculous, so contrary to the economic constructs of our world, that it begs us to question the very foundations upon which we build our understanding of wealth and poverty.

Why, then, do we find ourselves ensnared in a cycle of lack and excess? Could it be that we have strayed so far from the teachings of the old that we have rendered ourselves incapable of seeing the solution laid bare before us? As Jesus spoke in St. Luke 18:18-22, the path to life eternal involves a relinquishing of wealth, a surrender of the material in pursuit of the spiritual. It is a concept that shakes the very core of modern economics, yet it holds within it the potential for a world freed from the tyranny of poverty and death.

As you delve into the pages of this book, I urge you to approach with an open heart and a mind unburdened by preconceived notions. Allow yourself to be transported by the vivid imagery of scriptural wisdom, to be engaged by the direct questions that challenge the status quo. Let the rhythmic cadence of my words guide you through a narrative that is as much a saga of spiritual discovery as it is a treatise on economic revolution.

Through anecdotes and illustrations, I will show you the power of 'Diadidomi', not merely tell you. You will witness the stark contrast between the world as we know it and the world as it could be. And perhaps, in the quiet reflection between chapters, you will find yourself asking: is it possible that within this ancient Greek word lies the answer to the world's most pressing crisis?

1

———

THE PRINCIPLE OF DIADIDOMI

Diadidomi: The Divine Exchange

As the pen continues to dance across the pages of 'DIADIDOMI', a journey unfolds into the profound depths of a word that carries with it the weight of both spiritual inheritance and economic transformation. The Greek term 'Diadidomi', rooted in the ancient texts that have shaped the course of history, beckons us to explore its multifaceted meaning and the potential it holds to redefine the way we perceive and engage with the world's resources.

To truly grasp the essence of 'Diadidomi', one must venture beyond the superficial understanding of its translation as simply 'to give over' or 'to distribute'. The term encompasses more than the mere act of dispensing; it is an invitation to participate in a divine exchange, an economic dance that reflects the heavenly balance of abundance and need. It is the kind of giving that was demonstrated by the apostles in Acts 4:35, where they did not merely distribute alms, but rather they were conduits of a divine flow, channeling resources with an acute awareness of the community's heartbeat.

The quest for understanding beckons us to list the terms that serve as pillars upon which the meaning of 'Diadidomi' rests. These include 'giving', 'receiving', 'community', 'abundance', 'need', 'balance', and 'divine providence'. Each term, a gem in its own right, will be meticulously examined, revealing the multifaceted brilliance of a concept that transcends mere charity.

Giving, in its purest form, is an act of selflessness that enriches the soul as much as it supports the body. It is a voluntary transfer of something valuable from one individual to another, without the expectation of compensation. Receiving, often perceived as a passive act, is in truth an active engagement, an acceptance that honors the giver and completes the circle of generosity.

Community speaks to the interconnectedness of individuals, bound together by shared values, resources, and responsibilities. It is within this tapestry of human relations that 'Diadidomi' finds its most fertile ground. Abundance, contrary to the scarcity that haunts the nightmares of economists, is a state where resources exceed the immediate demands, allowing for the possibility of generous distribution.

The need is the counterpart to abundance, the hollow that yearns to be filled, the lack that beckons for a remedy. Balance is the harmonious point where abundance meets need, where the scales of divine providence are perfectly aligned. Divine providence, the overarching theme, is the belief that a higher power orchestrates the distribution of resources with perfect timing and wisdom.

But how do we tether these lofty concepts to the terra firma of the familiar? Perhaps we find parallels in the natural world; the way rain nourishes parched land or how a bee colony operates in selfless harmony, each member playing its role for the survival of the hive. Or maybe we recognize 'Diadidomi' in the simple acts of sharing a meal with a neighbor or donating time to mentor a young mind.

In the world of economics, 'Diadidomi' could be likened to the circulation of currency, where the flow of capital from investments to profits to wages and back again keeps the economy vibrant and alive. It is an intricate ballet of resources, akin to the exchange of oxygen and carbon dioxide in the lungs of the planet, where giving and receiving are as natural as breathing.

The intricate tapestry of 'Diadidomi' is not woven overnight. Like the masterful strokes of an artist, each term is painted with care, bringing forth a picture that invites contemplation. Is it possible that in the mundane acts of giving and receiving, we are participating in something far greater, a divine choreography that, if performed with intention, could alleviate the suffering of many?

This is not a journey for the faint of heart. It demands of us a willingness to look beyond the ledger and the stock ticker, to see the potential for a sacred economy that thrives on the principles of 'Diadidomi'. It calls for a bold reimagining of our social structures, a redefinition of wealth not as an accumulation of assets, but as the capacity to foster a flourishing community.

Through this exploration, we are not seeking answers that lie at the end of a neatly summarized conclusion. Instead, we are embarking on an expedition that meanders through the complex landscapes of spirituality and economics, guided by the constellations of ancient wisdom and modern understanding.

'Diadidomi' invites us into an exchange that transcends the material, an exchange that is as divine as it is human. Let us continue to weave the threads of this concept into the fabric of our collective consciousness, exploring the divine exchange that holds the promise of a transformed world.

Biblical Economics: Understanding Jesus' Miracle

In the verdant hills of Galilee, where the whispers of ancient prophecies mingled with the rustle of olive branches, a multitude gathered, hunger gnawing at their bellies and hope kindling in their hearts. They were drawn, as iron filings to a lodestone, by the teachings and miracles of a man whose words stirred the soul as much as they confounded the wise.

Jesus of Nazareth, the central figure of this unfolding narrative, stood before the weary travelers, his compassionate gaze sweeping over the sea of expectant faces. His disciples, a motley crew of fishermen, a tax collector, and others from walks of life as varied as the pebbles on the shore, flanked him, their faith a mixture of unwavering belief and human uncertainty.

The challenge that lay before them was as stark as the noonday sun: to feed a throng of five thousand with but five barley loaves and two small fishes. It was a task that defied human logic, a problem that would leave the greatest of minds bereft of solutions. And yet, amidst this impossibility, the air was thick with the scent of impending miracle.

Jesus' approach defied conventional strategies; it was neither the mobilization of scarce resources nor the rationing of supplies that one might expect in the face of such dire need. Instead, He offered thanks, a gesture of profound significance, and began to distribute the food through His disciples. It was an act of divine multiplication, a testament to the power of gratitude and trust in providence over the calculative parsimony of men.

As the bread and fish passed from hand to hand, a transformation occurred. What was once insufficient became more than enough, and the crowd was not just fed, but satisfied, with twelve baskets of surplus fragments collected afterward – a clear indication of the results, both material and spiritual, of this heavenly economics.

The analysis of this event must move beyond the surface, delving into the reflections it casts upon our understanding of scarcity and abundance. The miracle was not simply about the multiplication of food; it was a demonstration of an economy of the kingdom of God, where the rules of earthly economics are subverted by the principles of divine provision and generosity.

Visual aids, while absent from the textual records, can be imagined vividly: the breaking of bread, the distribution of fish, the satiation of the multitudes, and the gathering of the leftovers. These images serve as powerful metaphors for the economy of sufficiency that Jesus exemplified.

This singular event ties back to the greater narrative of 'DIA-DIDOMI', showcasing the very essence of divine distribution. It echoes the principles of community and balance, where the needs are met not by the accumulation of wealth, but through the sharing of resources, guided by a hand unseen yet ever-present.

And so, we find ourselves at the precipice of contemplation. Could our modern world, riddled with inequality and hunger, learn from this ancient tableau? How might we embody the principles of this biblical economy in our societies, businesses, and personal lives?

I, Kirk Anthony, having heard the voice of God and dedicated my life to the understanding of His divine principles, propose that within this miracle lies a blueprint for addressing the world's poverty. It is not through the amassing of wealth for the few but through the equitable distribution and trust in God's provision that we may find the solution to our most pressing economic woes.

The rhythm of this discourse, much like the cadence of a well-composed symphony, leads us to a crescendo of thought: In our pursuit of economic justice and abundance for all, might we be called to replicate not the accumulation, but the multiplication, as demonstrated on that Galilean hillside?

Let us ponder this question deeply. For in the answer, we may discover the key to unlocking a world where poverty is not an insurmountable challenge, but a problem already solved by the hands of He who fed the five thousand.

Macroeconomics and the Kingdom of God

As dawn breaks over the modern city's skyline, where steel and glass giants stand as monuments to human ingenuity and economic prowess, a question looms large: what if the underlying principles guiding these colossal structures were inspired by the divine economic model observed on the Galilean hillside? In a world of complex fiscal policies and global markets, can we find wisdom in the simplicity of the loaves and fishes?

Macroeconomics, the branch of economics concerned with large-scale or general economic factors, such as interest rates and national productivity, often operates on the axiom of scarcity. Resources are limited, and thus, their allocation must be managed with precision and strategy. Contrast this with the Kingdom of God, a biblical concept where providence reigns and abundance flows from the divine source. Herein lies our canvas for exploration, and it is on this tapestry that we shall weave our narrative, threading through the fabric of revelation and economics to propose a revolutionary economic model.

Why compare these seemingly disparate entities? The rationale is as compelling as it is urgent. In a world where economic disparity widens like a chasm, seeking a model that bridges the gap between prosperity and need is imperative. By examining the economy of God's kingdom, we might glean insights that could reshape our macroeconomic landscape.

We set our benchmarks for comparison: distribution of resources, the role of trust and gratitude, and the management of scarcity versus the assumption of abundance. These criteria will serve as the pillars upon which our analysis rests.

First, let us consider the distribution of resources. In macroeconomics, market mechanisms often dictate this distribution, with wealth tending to concentrate among the few. Meanwhile, the Kingdom of God operates on principles of equity and generosity, as exemplified by Jesus' feeding of the masses. Here, the similarity lies in the recognition of need; the contrast is in the response to that need.

Visually, imagine two graphs: one illustrating the lopsided bell curve of wealth distribution in modern society, the other depicting an even spread, as one might envisage the equal satisfaction of the crowd on that ancient hill. These images serve to crystallize the divergence in distributive methodologies.

What do these comparisons reveal? They unearth a profound truth: the macroeconomic system, bound by the tenets of scarcity, often fails to address the needs of the many. In contrast, the divine economy, anchored in abundance, ensures that needs are not just met but exceeded. This is not to suggest an impractical or utopian vision but to challenge the current paradigms that govern our distribution of resources.

The relevance to today's world is undeniable. We stand witness to a society where the gap between the wealthy and the impoverished widens daily. Yet, within this biblical example lies a paradigm that promotes both sustainability and sufficiency. It is here that we begin to see the outlines of a new economic model, one that dares to infuse macro-economic policies with the ethos of the divine economy.

Imagine a society where corporations, guided by principles of generosity and stewardship, invest in the well-being of communities. Ponder a financial system where trust and gratitude are not mere afterthoughts but foundational tenets that influence fiscal decisions. What kind of transformative impact could such an economy have on global poverty and inequality?

This line of questioning, infused with vivid imagery, is not intended to merely provoke reflection but to incite action. As we grapple with these questions, we unlock the potential for a radical reshaping of our economic landscape.

In conclusion, our journey from the macroeconomic towers to the biblical hillside has illuminated a path forward. Through the direct comparison and contrast of these two systems, we have uncovered a wealth of insights, each beckoning us to consider the broader implications of our economic choices. By integrating the principles of God's kingdom into our macroeconomic framework, we may yet craft an economy that mirrors not the scarcity of our fears but the abundance of our hopes.

Let us embrace this vision with a spirit of boldness. For in the melding of these realms lies the promise of a future where the bread of prosperity is not hoarded but shared, where the fish of opportunity multiply, leaving none behind.

May we have the courage to embark on this transformative journey, forging a new economic model that honors not just the wealth of the few, but the flourishing of all.

Alleviating Poverty: The Diadidomi Model

Poverty, like a shadow, stretches across nations and touches lives with a chilling hand. From sprawling cities where the destitute huddle in forgotten corners to rural expanses where families toil on barren land for meager yields, its reach is vast, and its grip, is relentless. In the face of such a pervasive challenge, one that threatens the very fabric of society, the quest for viable solutions becomes not just necessary, but urgent.

The specter of poverty is not merely a matter of empty bellies and threadbare clothing; it is a complex crisis that, left unchecked, can erode the foundations of communities and spawn a cycle of despair and degradation. What transpires if this plight goes unaddressed? Hunger gnaws at the potential of countless children, stifling their growth and aspirations. Education, a powerful lever for upliftment, becomes an unattainable dream. Communities crumble, and the chasm between the haves and the have-nots widens, undermining social cohesion and igniting unrest.

Amidst this bleak panorama, a beacon of hope emerges—the Diadidomi model. Rooted in an ancient Greek term meaning 'to give through,' this model embodies the ethos of communal sharing and unreserved generosity. It is a call to redefine wealth, not as an asset to be hoarded but as a resource to be shared, a means to empower and uplift, to rekindle the flame of hope where it has been extinguished by need.

But how does one translate such a lofty ideal into actionable steps? The implementation of the Diadidomi model requires a paradigm shift at both the micro and macro levels. It begins with the individual, with a personal commitment to share one's bounty with those less fortunate. It extends to businesses, urging them to invest a portion of their profits into community development projects. It encompasses governments, advocating for policies that facilitate rather than hinder the free flow of aid and support to those in need.

To animate this model, one might envision a community garden, a simple yet profound metaphor. Each member contributes what they can—seeds, labor, or water—and the harvest is shared among all. The garden thrives, and so do the people, sustained not only by the food it provides but also by the sense of purpose and camaraderie it fosters. This is Diadidomi in action, a tangible representation of its potential to transform lives.

The evidence of Diadidomi's efficacy can be found in small-scale initiatives that have yielded outsized impacts. Consider the village that pools resources to purchase a communal tractor, increasing agricultural productivity tenfold. Or the urban cooperative that provides microloans to its members, spurring entrepreneurship and self-reliance. These are not mere anecdotes; they are signposts pointing toward a path that, if followed, could lead to a future where poverty is not an insurmountable destiny but a challenge that can be overcome.

Of course, alternative solutions abound, each with its own merits and drawbacks. Some advocate for the rigorous application of free-market principles, arguing that economic growth alone can lift the masses from poverty. Others call for expansive welfare programs, funded by the state, to provide a safety net for the vulnerable. While these approaches have their place, they often fail to address the crux of the issue—the lack of a collective spirit of giving and mutual support that lies at the heart of Diadidomi.

Could it be that the answer to this age-old problem lies not in the cold calculus of economics but in the warm embrace of human kinship? Could we, as a society, dare to believe that by giving, we receive—not just materially, but spiritually and emotionally?

The journey toward eradicating poverty is fraught with challenges, but the Diadidomi model offers a roadmap that is at once idealistic and practical, rooted in the timeless virtues of compassion and community. It is a clarion call to look beyond our own needs and see the hunger in another's eyes, to extend a hand not in pity, but in solidarity.

In the final analysis, the measure of our humanity may well be determined by our willingness to embrace the Diadidomi philosophy, to enshrine the principles of sharing and generosity at the core of our endeavors. Let us cast aside the shackles of indifference and rise, together, to the noble task of lifting our fellow beings from the depths of poverty to the heights of shared prosperity.

In this spirit, let the pages that follow be not just a treatise on economics, but a manifesto for a movement that seeks to heal the world—one act of giving at a time.

Eternal Life Economics

In the annals of history, pivotal moments have often ignited the engines of change, reshaping the economic landscapes and the lives entwined with them. Picture the bustling markets of ancient Athens, where the concept of currency first found its footing, setting the stage for a revolution in trade and wealth distribution. Imagine the clamor of the Industrial Revolution, where mechanization birthed unprecedented productivity alongside stark disparities in wealth.

These milestones of progress, while advancing civilization, also cast long shadows of inequality and disenfranchisement. The chasm between the opulent lives of the few and the toiling existence of the many grew wider, prompting philosophers, theologians, and social reformers to seek solutions that might bridge this growing divide.

Fast forward to the present day, and the echoes of these historical shifts still reverberate through our global economy. The challenges we face are not just a reflection but a direct lineage of past trials: the struggle for equitable resource distribution, the battle against systemic poverty, and the quest for a sustainable model of shared prosperity.

Why, one might ask, is this historical tapestry crucial to our current predicament? Because without the knowledge of whence we came, we are adrift, unable to navigate the treacherous currents of modern economics. Only by understanding the lessons etched into history's ledger can we hope to craft solutions that are both innovative and enduring.

And so, we turn our gaze to Diadidomi, a philosophy that, while ancient in its roots, speaks to a timeless human truth—the intrinsic value of generosity and the transformative power of shared wealth. Could the principles of Diadidomi hold the key to bridging the gap between the pursuit of eternal life and the practicalities of earthly economics?

Consider the early Christian communities that practiced a form of Diadidomi, pooling resources and ensuring that none among them suffered want. These communities understood that their spiritual pursuit of eternal life was inextricably linked to their economic practices. They recognized that the health of their souls could not be separated from the well-being of their fellow beings.

How, then, does this ancient wisdom translate to our contemporary world, rife with its complex financial systems and digital economies? Are the tenets of Diadidomi merely idealistic relics, or do they contain pragmatic truths that we can apply to today's economic quandaries?

Let us delve into the heart of these questions, exploring the interplay between eternal values and temporal economies. Let us examine how the principles of Diadidomi can offer not just a salve for the wounds of poverty, but perhaps a new framework for economic interaction—one that values life in its fullest expression.

As we navigate the intricacies of this exploration, keep in mind the essence of Diadidomi: it is the act of giving that completes the cycle of receiving. It is a recognition that true wealth lies not in the hoarding of possessions but in the circulation of blessings. Could it be that the economy of eternal life—a life characterized by boundless love and generosity—is the ultimate model for our earthly endeavors?

With every transaction, every policy, every innovation, we are presented with a choice: to follow the well-trodden path of self-interest or to carve a new trail guided by the compass of communal well-being. The Diadidomi model challenges us to ask ourselves: What if the true measure of our economy's success was how well it provides for the least among us? Could we dare to imagine an economy that serves not just the present moment but the eternal continuum of our collective journey?

Through the following chapters, we shall embark on a quest to uncover the practical implications of integrating Diadidomi into the fabric of modern economic systems. We will seek to understand how the spirit of this ancient practice can be rekindled in an age of technological marvels and global interconnectivity.

As you turn each page, allow yourself to be transported into a realm of possibility where economics and eternity are not at odds but in harmony. Engage with the ideas presented, grapple with the challenges they pose, and envision the world that could emerge from the embrace of Eternal Life Economics—a world where every individual flourishes, and the wealth of the spirit reigns supreme.

2

———

THE SICKNESS OF POVERTY

The Roots of Poverty

In the fabric of human history, poverty weaves a persistent and complex thread, its pattern repeating yet ever-changing across the tapestry of time. Its roots run deep, and its branches, widespread, claw at civilizations, both ancient and modern, with indifferent cruelty. But how did this specter of scarcity and want first cast its long shadow over humanity?

At the dawn of civilization, as humanity took its first collective steps, there was no poverty as we understand it today. The earliest humans were hunter-gatherers, living in a world of relative abundance, where resources were shared within small communities. The concept of poverty emerged with the advent of agriculture and the subsequent division of labor. It was not merely the birth of farming but the inception of ownership that planted the seeds of poverty in the soil of human society.

As empires rose and fell, poverty's visage shifted with the sands of time. The ancient Egyptians, with their granaries full, still had peasants who toiled for a meager existence. In the glittering city-states of Greece, poverty coexisted with great wealth, philosophy, and democracy. And in Rome, even as the empire swelled with opulence and conquest, the chasm between the patricians and the plebeians grew ever wider.

Consider the visual of a Roman fresco, depicting the opulent lives of the elite, a stark contrast to the bone-thin figures of the beggars at their gates. Or the maps of medieval Europe, where feudal domains marked not just boundaries but the divide between lord and serf.

Moving through the ages, the Renaissance brought about a flourishing of art and thought, yet also saw the rise of the pauper class. The Industrial Revolution, a turning point in human productivity, forged disparate paths: immense wealth for some, and for others, the squalor of early factory life. Was it not Charles Dickens who painted the grim reality of poverty in Victorian England with such vivid strokes of his pen?

Across the ocean, the New World promised a fresh start, yet even there, the shadow of poverty fell upon both indigenous peoples and immigrant masses crowding into growing cities.

The Great Depression then served as a cruel reminder of poverty's tenacity, as breadlines snaked around city blocks.

What of cultural or regional variations, you ask? The story of poverty is not uniform across the globe. In some societies, the concept of community wealth persisted longer, while in others, colonization imposed new structures of economy and class that exacerbated the divide between rich and poor.

The modern era has seen attempts to redefine the narrative of poverty. Social safety nets, economic reforms, and international aid have all sought to lift the veil of want. Yet, the beast of poverty adapts, taking on new forms—urban slums, wage gaps, systemic inequalities. Today, poverty is not only measured by the lack of material wealth but by access to education, healthcare, and opportunities.

And what of the challenges, the controversies? Each step toward alleviating poverty seems to encounter resistance. Debates rage over the right approach: Is it through charity, policy reform, or economic growth? And what of the turning points? The recent pandemic has laid bare the fragility of progress, as millions slipped back below the poverty line, a sobering regression in the fight against want.

The Roots of Poverty are deep and gnarled, intertwining with our history and casting long shadows into our present. Can they be unearthed, can the ground be made fertile for all? Or is poverty an inextricable part of the human condition, a challenge that will forever test the limits of our empathy, our ingenuity, and our resolve?

Economic Disparity and Social Illness

In the midst of this historical panorama, where the specter of poverty looms like an uninvited ghost at the feast of progress, there lies an even more insidious ailment afflicting society: economic disparity. This is the chasm that stretches between the affluent and the impoverished, a divide that not only measures the distance between wealth and want but also mirrors the health of a society. Herein lies the crux of this book: to delve into the heart of how economic inequality festers and fuels societal maladies, eroding the quality of life for all.

Imagine a city, its skyline punctured by gleaming towers of glass and steel, a testament to human ingenuity and ambition. Yet, in the shadow of these monuments to wealth, there are neighborhoods where the air hangs heavy with despair. Here, the streets tell a different story—one of struggle, neglect, and a yearning for equality. This stark dichotomy is not penned by chance but is the byproduct of a system where the scales of prosperity are imbalanced.

The impact of this economic imbalance is profound and far-reaching. Consider education, the bedrock of opportunity. In affluent neighborhoods, schools boast state-of-the-art facilities and a plethora of resources. A short distance away, in communities less favored by fortune, schools crumble, textbooks are shared, and teachers are overburdened. How can we, as a society, stand idly by while the future of our children is determined not by their potential but by their postal code?

To personalize this issue, take the story of Maria, a single mother of three in a bustling metropolis. Maria works two jobs, yet the specter of poverty is a constant companion in her cramped apartment. Her children, bright and eager to learn, are stifled by overcrowded classrooms and outdated materials. Maria's story is not unique; it is echoed in millions of households where the dream of upward mobility is eclipsed by the harsh reality of economic stagnation.

And what are the stakes? They are nothing less than the fabric of our society. When the middle class erodes and the gap between the rich and the poor widens, social cohesion unravels. Crime rates escalate, public health suffers, and political unrest simmers. This is not mere speculation, but the verdict of history, repeated in countless studies and reports. The question we must ask ourselves is, can we afford to ignore the perils of such disparity?

The path ahead, while fraught with challenges, is also lined with hope. This book will guide you through the maze of economic inequality, illuminating the ways in which policy, education, and community engagement can serve as beacons to a fairer and more just society. Solutions such as progressive taxation, universal basic income, and equitable education funding will be explored, not as panaceas, but as steps toward bridging the divide.

As we embark on this journey through the pages ahead, consider the role each of us plays in either perpetuating or challenging the status quo. Are we content to be mere bystanders in the theater of inequality, or will we take up the mantle of change? It is only through collective action and a renewed commitment to the common good that we can hope to heal the social illnesses wrought by economic disparity.

In the chapters to come, you will encounter the voices of economists, educators, policymakers, and those living on the frontline of this battle. Their stories and insights will weave a narrative that is both enlightening and galvanizing. As you turn each page, remember that the journey toward a more equitable world is not a sprint but a marathon—it requires endurance, resilience, and an unwavering belief in the possibility of change.

Economic Disparity and Social Illness is not just a book; it is a call to arms. It is an invitation to look beyond the statistics and see the human faces of inequality. It is a challenge to dismantle the barriers that divide us and to build, in their stead, bridges of understanding and cooperation. Together, we can redefine the future and ensure that prosperity is not a privilege of the few but the right of the many.

The Diadidomi Cure

At the heart of the Diadidomi philosophy lies a transformative vision, one that sees beyond the constraints of our current economic paradigms and toward a horizon where poverty is not just alleviated but eradicated. The term 'Diadidomi', of ancient provenance, signifies the act of giving through and through, encapsulating the ethos of reciprocal generosity and shared prosperity. It is with this spirit that we embark upon a journey to redefine wealth and its distribution, guided not only by systemic changes but also by profound spiritual insights.

Our journey begins with a clear objective: to harness the power of Diadidomi to create a world where every individual has the means to live with dignity, access to opportunities, and the ability to contribute meaningfully to society. The eradication of poverty is not merely a lofty dream, but a tangible goal within our grasp.

To achieve this end, we must first gather the necessary materials or prerequisites: a deep understanding of the current economic system, a willingness to embrace new paradigms of wealth distribution, and a commitment to personal and communal growth. Additionally, we require a network of like-minded individuals, organizations, and governments willing to pioneer and implement the principles of Diadidomi.

A broad overview of our roadmap presents a series of transformative steps: the cultivation of a Diadidomi mindset, the restructuring of economic models, the implementation of equitable education and healthcare systems, and the fostering of community-driven development.

Delving into detailed steps, we begin with the cultivation of a Diadidomi mindset. This involves a shift in perspective, from viewing wealth as a finite resource to be hoarded, to seeing it as a renewable energy to be shared. It includes nurturing empathy and understanding the interconnectedness of all life. Such a mindset prepares us for the systemic changes necessary to distribute wealth in a manner that benefits all.

The restructuring of economic models is our next detailed phase. This entails the adoption of policies that prioritize the well-being of people and the planet over profit. Measures such as progressive taxation, universal basic income, and the promotion of cooperative business models fall under this category. These are not mere tweaks to the existing system but foundational changes that align with the principles of Diadidomi.

To offer tips and warnings, it is imperative we move with caution and foresight. Change of this magnitude will encounter resistance. It is crucial to build strong coalitions and anticipate the challenges posed by entrenched interests. Moreover, we must ensure that the transition to a Diadidomi-based economy does not create new forms of exclusion or inequality.

Testing or validation of our efforts comes through measurable outcomes: reduced poverty rates, narrower income gaps, improved access to quality education and healthcare, and increased community vitality. These indicators will not only show progress but also inspire further action.

For those facing challenges in implementing the Diadidomi Cure, troubleshooting becomes essential. Common problems may include a lack of political will, economic backlash, or societal skepticism. Solutions are found in persistent advocacy, public education, and the demonstration of successful models that can be replicated.

Now, as we ponder this path, can we not see ourselves as architects of a new dawn? Will you, dear reader, join hands in this noble enterprise? Imagine the radiant world that could emerge from the seeds we plant today.

Let us not be lulled into inaction by the siren song of complacency, for the stakes are too high. Instead, let us rise, with hearts aflame with the spirit of Diadidomi, to weave a tapestry of justice and abundance. In this quest, our guide is the unshakable belief that, together, we can reshape the contours of destiny and gift our children a legacy of hope.

As we move through the pages of this discourse, remember that the road to a Diadidomi world is paved with both intention and action. It is a journey that beckons each of us to leave an indelible mark on the annals of time, transforming 'what is' into 'what ought to be'.

This, then, is the essence of The Diadidomi Cure—a manifesto for a future where poverty is but a distant memory, and prosperity is the shared song of humanity. Let us march forward, with the torch of Diadidomi lighting our way, to a summit where every soul can bask in the warmth of abundance and peace.

Testimonies of Transformation

Under the warm embrace of the African sun, the village of Moyo came to life with the crowing of roosters and the rhythmic pounding of grain. Among the thatched roofs and mud-brick walls, a narrative of hope was unfolding—a story not of an individual, but of an entire community that had begun to dance to the beat of Diadidomi.

In the heart of this village stood a woman named Amina, her silhouette etched against the dawn as she walked toward the communal well. Her gait, once weighed down by despair, now carried the lightness of someone who had glimpsed a future brimming with possibilities. The lines on her face, each a testament to a hardship endured, seemed to soften with each passing day, as her community embraced a new way of life.

Amina was not always a believer in the power of shared prosperity. The concept of Diadidomi, with its promise of mutual support and collective growth, had seemed as distant as the city skylines to a villager like her. Yet, it was in the very essence of her daily struggles—the relentless fight against poverty and the silent prayers for her children's future—that the seeds of transformation were sown.

As the days unfolded, the villagers of Moyo began to witness a change. It started with the formation of a cooperative, a gathering of souls determined to pool their resources and knowledge. They planted crops with shared labor, traded skills for goods, and, most importantly, they learned to give as much as they received. The cooperative was not merely an economic endeavor; it was the embodiment of Diadidomi, a living, breathing example of the wisdom that had been passed down to them.

Could it be, Amina pondered, that the answer to their prayers had been nestled within their collective spirit all along? The cooperative's success was not just measured in the surplus of crops but in the newfound confidence that shone in the eyes of her neighbors. Children who once spent their days toiling in fields now sat in makeshift classrooms, their laughter a melody that harmonized with the chirping of birds.

But the journey was not without its perils. The specter of doubt lingered, whispering fears of failure and scarcity. How could a small village, seemingly insignificant in the grand tapestry of the world, sustain such a utopian ideal? The answer came not in words but in deeds—the selfless acts that bound the community together, the unwavering belief that every contribution mattered, and the realization that the strength of Diadidomi lay in its very simplicity.

Amidst this blossoming of collective will, a visitor arrived in Moyo. His name was Dr. Tobias, a man whose life's work had been dedicated to the study of economic models that transcended traditional boundaries. He had heard of Moyo's experiment with Diadidomi and had come to bear witness to its effects.

"Tell me," Dr. Tobias inquired one evening as the villagers gathered around a fire, the flames casting a warm glow on their hopeful faces, "what has been the greatest lesson you've learned from this endeavor?"

An elder, his face etched with the wisdom of years, spoke up. "That wealth is not measured in coins or crops alone, but in the richness of our relationships. That prosperity is a collective song, each of us contributing a note to its melody."

Dr. Tobias nodded, his eyes reflecting the fire's light and the truth in the elder's words. He knew that the stories of Moyo would resonate far beyond the boundaries of the village, echoing a universal truth that had the power to transform societies.

As the night deepened and the stars blinked into existence above, Amina's heart swelled with a sense of purpose. The path ahead was still shrouded in uncertainty, but the villagers of Moyo had become wayfarers on a journey of shared destiny, their footsteps guided by the principles of Diadidomi.

And so, dear reader, as you delve into the pages that follow, consider this: might you find inspiration in the story of Moyo? Will you dare to envision a world where the act of giving becomes the cornerstone of our existence? The wisdom of Diadidomi is not confined to the pages of a book or the borders of a village; it is a call to action that resonates in the heart of every human being.

Let us embrace this wisdom, for in it lies the key to a future where transformation is not just a testimony but a tangible reality for all. As Kirk Anthony, a man who has dedicated his life to the pursuit of spiritual and economic enlightenment, I invite you to join me on this journey of discovery and to become a part of the Diadidomi legacy that we can build together.

From Survival to Thriving

As you turn the pages of this journey, I, Kirk Anthony, extend to you a promise that is as audacious as it is essential. This book will not merely provide you with an understanding of the Diadidomi principles but will also empower you with the tools to transform your existence. It is more than a narrative; it is an invitation to a revolution of the soul and society.

Imagine a world where scarcity is but a shadow of the past,

where abundance flows as naturally as the rivers that carve the earth. The Diadidomi principles are the bedrock of this flourishing reality, a system that celebrates the power of giving, receiving, and regenerating wealth in all its forms. Here, within these chapters, lie the methodologies that have turned barren fields into bountiful gardens, and despairing hearts into fountains of hope.

You may wonder, how can such a utopian vision be attainable. How can principles that seem as ancient as the earth itself hold the key to modern prosperity? Doubts may cloud your mind, like the mist that veils the dawn. Yet, consider my own journey: from hearing the divine at a tender age, excelling through academia, and serving my nation with honor, to founding an institution devoted to the fusion of spiritual insight and economic foresight. My life is a testament to the power of faith and the tangible results of applying the Diadidomi ethos.

The transformation awaits, and it beckons you with open arms. Envision yourself not just surviving, but thriving. Picture a life unshackled from the relentless pursuit of mere existence, where each day is a fresh canvas painted with the vibrant colors of shared success and joy. This book will be your guide, your mentor, alongside you as you embark on a path that few have trodden, but all have longed for.

Consider this a covenant between you, the reader, and the profound wisdom held within these pages. The value you will glean here is not just in the intellectual understanding but in the awakening of a new consciousness. A consciousness that sees beyond the self, recognizes our interconnectedness, and champions a collective ascent to heights yet unimagined.

Is your spirit stirred? Does the prospect of such an existence ignite a fire within you? Let that flame be your beacon as you traverse the landscape of Diadidomi. For in this book lies not merely words, but seeds. Seeds that, when sown in the fertile ground of your will and action, will yield a harvest beyond what you have dared to dream.

The journey of Moyo is your journey too. A journey from survival to thriving. From the individual to the collective. From the finite to the infinite. Take the first step, and let us walk together toward a horizon that grows brighter with each act of giving, each moment of sharing, and each heartbeat of a humanity united in purpose and prosperity.

Your guide,

Kirk Anthony

3

SPIRITUAL MICROECONOMICS

Small Acts, Big Impact

In a world seemingly governed by the ominous clouds of economic disparity and societal unrest, the concept of Diadidomi—translated from the ancient Greek as "to give through"—stood like a beacon of hope. It was in the quaint, cobblestoned streets of Pireas, a bustling port town in Greece, where this paradigm of sharing and circulation of wealth would find fertile ground for an extraordinary transformation.

As the sun nestled against the horizon, painting a watercolor of oranges and pinks across the sky, the locals of Pireas closed their shops for the day. However, for Eleni Georgiou, a small bakery owner, the day was far from over. Her oven still radiated warmth, and the scent of freshly baked bread lingered in the air. Beside her, Nikos, a fisherman whose rough hands spoke of the sea's embrace, shared stories of the day's catch.

Eleni and Nikos were the main players in a movement that would soon capture the hearts and minds of this community. Eleni, with her infectious smile and knack for kneading dough into loaves of hope, had long been a cornerstone of the Pireas economy. Nikos, with his intimate knowledge of the sea's ebb and flow, provided sustenance for many locals. Yet, both faced a similar challenge: the economic downturn had left their businesses—and their customers—struggling.

The problem was clear: fewer people could afford daily bread or fresh fish, and even fewer could patronize other local businesses. The ripple effects were causing the community's economic fabric to fray at the edges.

The solution came on a day when Eleni noticed an elderly man count out his coins, his hands trembling, unsure if he had enough to afford his meal. Moved by this, she offered him a loaf of bread in the house. "Share it with someone," she said, her voice a mixture of kindness and resolve. This simple act of generosity sparked an idea. What if businesses in Pireas adopted a system where customers could pay forward goods or services to those in need?

The strategy began with Eleni and Nikos. They started a "Diadidomi Board" in their establishments where customers could purchase an additional item for someone less fortunate. A loaf of bread, a cup of coffee, or a fresh catch from

Nikos' boat could be claimed by anyone in need, no questions asked.

The results were nothing short of miraculous. Within months, the Diadidomi Board became a symbol of community resilience. Individuals from all walks of life participated, and as they did, something remarkable happened: the local economy began to see signs of recovery. People who claimed the acts of kindness often found ways to contribute themselves, leading to a revitalized cycle of giving and spending.

Upon reflection, the impact of this approach was multi-fold. While the data showed an uptick in overall sales and a decrease in local poverty rates, the less tangible results were equally profound. The spirit of generosity fostered a deeper sense of community, trust, and mutual support that statistics could scarcely convey.

Visual aids, such as photographs of the Diadidomi Board brimming with post-it notes of paid-forward items, adorned the walls of Eleni's bakery and Nikos' fish market. These images served as powerful reminders of the collective goodwill.

This small act of kindness in Pireas was not just a local anecdote; it was a microcosm of the larger narrative of Diadidomi. It demonstrated how a simple, yet profound, economic action could ripple outward, fostering societal transformations far beyond what one might expect from such humble beginnings.

As the chapter draws to a close, one can't help but ponder: What if this model were replicated on a larger scale? Could the principles of Diadidomi offer a blueprint for healing the economic divides that plague modern societies?

With the turn of every page, the story of Pireas invites readers to not just witness but to partake in the movement of Diadidomi. It's a call to action, a question that yearns for an answer—how might we, through small acts of generosity, forge a path toward a more equitable and united world?

In the silence that follows, where the echo of this question lingers, the reader is left to contemplate their role in the tapestry of change, woven one small act at a time.

Miracle of Multiplication

When one ponders the ancient texts, it is not uncommon to stumble upon narratives of wonder and transcendence. Among them, the story of Jesus feeding the multitudes with but five loaves of bread and two fish stands as a testament to the power of faith and the concept of abundance. Yet, beneath the surface of this miraculous event lies a tapestry of microeconomic principles that, when unfurled, reveal insights as applicable today as they were two millennia ago.

The notion of multiplication, particularly within the realm of microeconomics, is one that speaks of the ability to generate more from less. It speaks to the heart of resource allocation, the efficiency of distribution, and the power of collective contribution. The miracle, in its essence, could be seen as a metaphor for the potential that lies in shared resources and community-led efforts to address scarcity.

In breaking down the event, one must first understand the principle of scarcity, an incontrovertible truth within economics. Resources are limited, and their allocation often determines the vitality or decline of a community. The loaves and fish were scarce, yet the distribution methodology employed in the miracle ensured that this scarcity was not only overcome but was transformed into a surplus.

The strategy was simple and yet profound: the little that was available was shared among many, not by diluting the individual portions but by some inexplicable amplification. In today's terms, we might equate this to the impact of social welfare programs or the dynamic power of crowdfunding platforms. Each, in its own right, takes a pool of modest contributions and amplifies their effect to meet the needs of a larger community.

Consider the modern-day example of a food bank. Here, donations from individuals and businesses converge, creating a repository from which those in need can draw sustenance. This is the practical application of the multiplication concept. It's the transformation of individual acts of giving into a collective resource that has the power to sustain many.

Moreover, the miracle's setting provides a lens through which to view the concept of economies of scale. As the food was distributed, the act of breaking bread and sharing fish became a decentralized process, with each small group managing their allocation effectively. This mirrors how smaller, localized economies can benefit from managing resources at a scale that reduces waste and increases efficiency.

It is also impossible to ignore the psychological and sociological dimensions intertwined with the economic. The generosity on display could have a ripple effect, encouraging others to contribute, thus creating a virtuous cycle of giving and receiving. Studies have shown that acts of kindness can indeed stimulate further acts of generosity within communities, a phenomenon which, in the long term, can lead to greater economic resilience.

One must also consider the complexities of valuation. How does one measure the worth of a loaf of bread or a fish when it becomes not just a meal but a symbol of hope? In this context, the intrinsic value of the food items transcended their market price, embedding within them a value that was both communal and deeply personal.

Yet, in the clarity of hindsight, we must ask direct questions: How can we replicate such an economy of abundance in a world that seems to revolve around competition and individual gain? Can the principles of shared resources and community resilience be scaled up to address the systemic challenges of our time?

The story of the loaves and fishes may not provide all the answers, but it certainly offers a framework for reimagining our approach to economic disparity. It suggests that the act of giving, when multiplied across a network of willing participants, can lead to outcomes that exceed the sum of their parts.

In conclusion, the key takeaways from this ancient narrative are manifold. It challenges us to rethink the nature of scarcity, to recognize the potential in collective action, and to see generosity not as a finite resource but as a catalyst for economic transformation. It invites us to consider the power of economies of scale, the psychological impact of giving, and the true value of the resources we so often take for granted.

As the story of the miracle fades and the realities of our economic landscape loom large, we are left to ponder how we might apply these lessons to our own communities. Could it be that within the folds of this ancient miracle, we find the blueprint for a modern-day economic resurrection? Could a community's willingness to embrace the principles of Diadidomi be the first step toward a miracle of multiplication in our own time?

And so, with these reflections, this chapter closes, not with an ending but with an invitation—an invitation to multiply our efforts, to share our resources, and to believe in the transformative power of community. For it is in this collective embrace that we might just find the miracle we seek.

Spiritual Capital in Action

In the labyrinth of economic theories and practices, one concept that emerges with an ethereal glow is that of spiritual capital. Its essence lies not in the tangible, but in the intangible qualities of our interactions, values, and beliefs. To understand its significance in the realms of personal growth and community development, we must begin by untangling the threads of its definition, exploring its dimensions, and connecting these with the concrete examples that ground us in our shared reality.

As we delve into this exploration, we recognize that the foundation of comprehension rests upon the clarification of terms. A term, after all, is a beacon of meaning, casting light upon the concepts it signifies. In this journey, we shall illuminate the terms 'spiritual capital,' 'personal economic development,' and 'community economic development,' weaving a tapestry of understanding that binds the ethereal to the earthly.

The term 'spiritual capital' is often shrouded in ambiguity, its contours elusive to those uninitiated in its depths. At its core, spiritual capital encompasses the wealth of resources emanating from our spiritual beliefs and practices. It is the reservoir of virtues, ethics, and moral commitments that individuals and communities draw upon in times of decision-making and action.

Personal economic development, on the other hand, is a more familiar phrase. It refers to the process by which individuals enhance their economic status and well-being, often through education, skill acquisition, and the judicious management of financial resources. Here, the focus is on the individual's journey to financial stability and prosperity.

Community economic development, while echoing personal economic development in its objectives of improved well-being, extends beyond the individual. It involves collective efforts to create economic opportunities that benefit a community, with strategies that may include supporting local businesses, fostering job creation, and improving local infrastructure.

One might wonder, how does spiritual capital manifest in the context of personal and community economic development? Imagine a gardener, tending to the soil with care, planting seeds with hope, and nurturing growth with patience. This gardener possesses not only the knowledge of horticulture but also the virtues of diligence, foresight, and a sense of connection to the earth. These virtues, intangible as they may be, are the spiritual capital at work, guiding the hands that till the soil.

In the sphere of personal economic development, spiritual capital is the fortitude that drives an individual to seek knowledge, the resilience in the face of adversity, and the ethics that shape business dealings. It is what compels one to save for the future, invest with caution, and share wealth with generosity. Beyond the balance sheet, it is the spiritual capital that informs choices, ensuring they are not only financially sound but also morally grounded.

When we shift our gaze to the broader horizon of community economic development, spiritual capital reveals itself in the collective conscience of a people. It is present in the trust between neighbors, the shared commitment to the common good, and the cultural narratives that inspire unity and collaboration. It is the invisible hand that guides communal projects, the spirit of volunteerism, and the ethical frameworks that underpin fair trade and sustainable practices.

Consider, for instance, the cooperative movement, where individuals unite under shared goals and values to create economic structures that serve their community. Here, spiritual capital is the glue that binds members in mutual trust and common purpose, driving the cooperative to thrive not only economically but also as a model of ethical business practice.

Yet, amidst these discussions, one may pause and ponder, how we nurture this spiritual capital. How do we ensure its flow and growth within the intricate channels of our economic systems? These questions beckon us to look inward, to reflect on our values, and to engage in actions that resonate with our deepest convictions.

The nurturing of spiritual capital begins with the individual, in the quiet contemplation of what truly matters, in the daily choices that align with one's values, and in the cultivation of relationships that are enriched with meaning and purpose. From this personal foundation, spiritual capital blossoms outward, influencing communities through acts of kindness, ethical leadership, and the promotion of social justice.

In this exploration of spiritual capital, we have traversed from definitions to real-world applications, from the individual's internal landscape to the collective external reality. We have seen how the intangible qualities of our spirit weave through the very fabric of our economic lives, shaping decisions, fueling progress, and fostering a sense of shared destiny.

This discourse on spiritual capital is not an end in itself but rather an invitation to a deeper engagement with the values that underpin our economic interactions. It beckons us to recognize the power of our spiritual resources, to harness them for the enrichment of our personal lives, and to mobilize them for the advancement of our communities. In the grand theatre of economics, spiritual capital takes center stage, not as a silent specter, but as a dynamic force that shapes the narrative of our collective journey.

Econometrics of Generosity

In a world where numbers dictate narratives and data drives decisions, the study of generosity finds its quantifiable muse in the field of econometrics. This branch of economics, wielding statistical methods and mathematical models, seeks to decode the intricacies of human behavior and its impact on the broader economy. The concept of 'Diadidomi,' a term derived from ancient Greek meaning 'to give through,' offers a unique lens through which the effects of generosity can be scrutinized, measured, and understood.

At the heart of this exploration lies a profound assertion: that generosity is not merely an altruistic gesture but a significant economic force capable of influencing markets, shaping policy, and transforming societies. It is a claim that challenges the conventional wisdom of self-interest as the primary driver of economic activity and posits that the act of giving possesses its own utility, both for the donor and the recipient.

The primary evidence supporting this claim comes from a myriad of studies that trace the flow of generosity and its ripple effects across communities. One such study examines the impact of charitable donations on local economies, revealing that for every dollar donated, there is a multiplier effect that significantly exceeds the initial contribution. This phenomenon, akin to the spreading of seeds by a sower, sees the act of giving as the catalyst for a cycle of economic activity that benefits a multitude of stakeholders.

Digging deeper into this evidence, we find that generosity stimulates economic growth in several ways. It can boost consumer spending, as recipients of charitable acts often redirect their newfound resources toward goods and services. It also encourages investment in community projects and infrastructures, fostering an environment conducive to business development and entrepreneurial innovation. Moreover, the act of giving engenders a sense of social cohesion and trust, intangible assets that are critical for the smooth functioning of any economy.

As compelling as this narrative may be, there are counterarguments to consider. Skeptics point out instances where generosity may lead to dependency, discouraging self-reliance and innovation. Others argue that the resources allocated to charitable causes might be more efficiently utilized if invested directly into businesses or technological advancements. These counterpoints present a nuanced view, reminding us that generosity, like any economic variable, has its limitations and potential downsides.

In response, a clarification emerges: generosity must be strategic and mindful. Philanthropy, when applied with foresight and aligned with sustainable development goals, can empower communities rather than render them dependent. This strategic approach to giving ensures that the seeds sown today will bear fruit in the form of self-sustaining systems and empowered individuals capable of contributing to the economy in the long term.

Further supporting the initial claim is the evidence of generosity's impact on mental health and, by extension, productivity. Studies have shown that individuals who engage in acts of giving experience increased levels of happiness and satisfaction. This positive psychological state can translate into higher work performance, reduced absenteeism, and greater organizational commitment—all factors that contribute to a more dynamic and productive economy.

In the final assessment, the conclusion is clear: generosity, when understood through the lens of econometrics and practiced with intention, is not merely a moral imperative but an economic catalyst. It is a force that, when harnessed, has the power to ignite cycles of growth, foster innovation, and build resilient communities. The evidence presented herein underscores the validity of the claim that generosity is an indispensable component of a thriving economy, and Diadidomi serves as a model for its application.

In the pages that follow, we will continue to unravel the complexities of generosity within the economic sphere, examining its multifaceted impacts and the policies that can amplify its positive outcomes. Generosity, in its most enlightened form, is a gift that keeps on giving—a truth that the econometrics of generosity lays bare for all to see.

The Power of Giving

The late afternoon sun cast a warm glow over the small town as Marianne stepped out of her quaint flower shop, her arms laden with bouquets of vibrant tulips and roses. The town square was alive with the sounds of laughter and conversation, a tapestry of community life unfolding before her. Children played near the fountain, their parents watching from nearby benches, enjoying the simple pleasure of a peaceful moment.

At the heart of this scene stood an elderly man, Mr. Hernandez, known to all as the benevolent soul who had once been a cornerstone of local commerce. With his once-thriving bakery now closed, his days were spent sharing stories with passersby, his eyes reflecting the wisdom of experience and the kindness that had defined his life.

Marianne approached Mr. Hernandez, her stride purposeful, her expression a blend of determination and warmth. The bouquets in her hands were not for sale; they were her gift to the town's unsung hero. As she handed the flowers to Mr. Hernandez, the surprise and joy in his eyes were mirrored in her own. "For the countless loaves of bread you've given away to those in need," she said, her voice tinged with respect.

The act of giving, simple yet profound, set off a chain of events that rippled through the town. Inspired by Marianne's generosity, others began to contribute in their own ways.

The local carpenter repaired a widow's broken fence without charge; a group of teenagers organized a cleanup of the town park, their youthful energy breathing new life into the community space.

These stories, each a thread in the rich tapestry of Diadidomi, illuminated the transformative power of giving. Marianne's gesture was not merely an act of personal kindness; it was a catalyst that sparked a movement, a testament to the profound effects of selfless generosity.

But why do we give? What compels us to reach out to others, often at the expense of our own comfort? Beneath the surface of these questions lies a universal truth: the act of giving transcends the immediate exchange. It is an affirmation of connection, a recognition that our fates are intertwined, that the well-being of our neighbor is inseparable from our own.

Is it possible, then, that the power of giving lies not in the act itself but in the bonds it fortifies? As we delve deeper into the myriad ways in which generosity shapes our lives, we uncover a wealth of wisdom waiting to be embraced. We learn that giving is not a one-way street but a journey of mutual enrichment, a path that leads both giver and receiver to a place of greater understanding and fulfillment.

Consider the tale of Marianne and Mr. Hernandez. What began as a single act of kindness soon blossomed into a communal endeavor, each participant discovering the joy of contribution. Their experiences echo a profound lesson: that generosity begets generosity, that the seeds of compassion, once sown, can yield a harvest of goodwill that sustains us all.

As we explore these stories, we see the unmistakable signs of a deeper truth: that generosity, in its purest form, is an expression of love. It is a force that knows no bounds, transcending barriers of age, culture, and circumstance. It is a light that, once kindled, can illuminate the darkest corners of our world.

In the pages that follow, we will journey together through the landscapes of giving, encountering souls whose lives have been touched by the spirit of Diadidomi. We will witness acts of breathtaking selflessness and uncover the lessons they impart. We will discover that the power of giving is not merely an ideal to aspire to but a reality to be lived, a beacon that guides us toward a more compassionate and connected existence.

And so, dear reader, I invite you to take the first step on this journey, to open your heart to the stories that await. For in the act of giving, we find the essence of our humanity, and in its embrace, we discover the true meaning of wealth. Let us embark on this path together, with open hands and open hearts, for it is in giving that we receive the greatest gift of all: the realization that we are all keepers of each other's joy.

4

CONQUERING THE SIN OF GREED

Greed: A Global Epidemic

In the modern age, where technological advancements and globalization have reshaped the contours of our societies, a specter haunts the collective consciousness—greed. This insidious force has infiltrated every level of human interaction, from the individual's pursuit of wealth to the machinations of multinational corporations. The disparity between the haves and the have-nots widens, and with it, the very fabric of our global community stretches thin, threatening to tear under the weight of unchecked desire.

How did we arrive at this juncture where the accumulation of wealth takes precedence over the welfare of the many? The answer lies not in economics alone but in the heart of human nature—where the seed of greed germinates and flourishes in the fertile soil of opportunity.

Consider the impact of this greed. It manifests in environmental degradation, as pristine forests fall to the axe of profit, and in socio-economic inequality, where a single individual amasses the wealth of nations while millions languish in poverty. This is not merely an issue of moral posturing; it is a crisis that erodes the very pillars of our civilization, undermining democracy, social cohesion, and the sustainability of life on our planet.

Yet, the gravity of the situation comes into sharper relief through the lens of personal narrative. Take, for instance, the story of Maria, a mother of three in a developing nation, whose ancestral lands were appropriated by a multinational seeking to exploit the local resources. Her family's livelihood was devastated, their community disintegrated, and their cultural heritage relegated to the margins of history—all for the sake of swelling corporate coffers.

The stakes are monumental. If our collective greed continues to go unchecked, it will not only deepen existing inequalities but also sow the seeds of conflict, both within and between nations. It is a harbinger of a dystopian future where the many serve the few, and the planet lays ravaged and barren, a casualty of an insatiable appetite for more.

But what if there is a way forward—a path that leads us away from this precipice? This book will serve as a compass, guiding readers through the labyrinth of avarice to emerge into a landscape of sustainable prosperity and equitable distribution. It will lay bare the mechanisms of greed, but more importantly, it will illuminate the strategies by which we can rehabilitate our economies, our societies, and our individual values.

In the chapters that follow, we will explore the philosophical underpinnings of desire and the historical trajectories that have brought us to this point. We will dissect the policies that enable and exacerbate greed, and we will shine a light on the grassroots movements and innovative thinkers who are forging new paradigms. This is not just an academic exploration—it is a call to arms, an invitation to join a burgeoning revolution of thought and action.

Can we not envision a world where wealth serves the common good, rather than the other way around? Where the measure of a society's success is not its GDP but the well-being of its people? It is within our grasp to recalibrate our priorities, to foster a culture of generosity and stewardship. The solutions we will propose are not merely theoretical constructs; they are practical, actionable, and, most importantly, rooted in the reality of human potential.

The journey to a more equitable future is fraught with challenges, but it is a journey we must undertake. The alternative is to continue down the path of self-destruction, driven by the insatiable engine of greed.

This book is your guide through the wilderness of excess and exploitation. It is a beacon of hope that illuminates a path to a world where greed is not the epidemic but the anomaly. Are you ready to take the first step?

Moral Economics

Understanding the essence of moral economics necessitates grappling with a lexicon that, while potentially unfamiliar, forms the bedrock of a more equitable society. The concepts enshrined within this terminology are not mere abstractions; they are the sinews and muscles that could move the world toward a vision of shared prosperity and social justice. Their meaning, contextualized within the teachings of Diadidomi, offers a blueprint for a world unshackled from the chains of greed.

As we embark on this intellectual voyage, it becomes imperative to anchor our thoughts in the clarity of precise definitions. These terms are the stars by which we will navigate the turbulent seas of economic reform. They are the keys that unlock the door to understanding, and with understanding comes the power to transform.

The terms we shall explore include altruism, sustainable growth, community investment, ethical consumerism, social entrepreneurship, and wealth redistribution. Each word, a vessel of profound importance, carries within it the potential to redefine the trajectory of our global economy.

Altruism, derived from the Latin word 'alteri' or 'other', is the selfless concern for the well-being of others. It is the antithesis of greed, a beacon of hope in a world darkened by the shadows of self-interest. Altruism is not just an ideal; it's a tangible practice that manifests in acts of generosity and collaboration. Real-world examples abound, from the individual who donates their time and resources to help those in need, to the corporation that prioritizes social responsibility over profit maximization.

Sustainable growth, a term often bandied about with little regard for its profound implications, refers to economic development that meets present needs without compromising the ability of future generations to meet theirs. It is the golden mean between stagnation and unchecked expansion. Consider a forest managed sustainably: it provides wood for our needs while maintaining its ecological integrity for the wildlife it shelters and the generations that will follow us.

Community investment is the deployment of resources to improve the well-being of a particular geographical area. It is a concept rooted in the belief that the prosperity of the individual is inextricably linked to the prosperity of the collective. One need only look to the rejuvenation of urban centers, where local businesses thrive thanks to the support of their communities, to see this principle in action.

Ethical consumerism stands as a vanguard against the rampant materialism that fuels greed. It is the practice of purchasing products that are ethically produced, that does not harm the environment, and that support fair labor practices. By choosing fair-trade coffee, consumers send ripples across the globe, affirming their solidarity with the farmers who toiled to harvest the beans.

Social entrepreneurship is the art of marrying innovation with a social mission. Social entrepreneurs are the alchemists of the business world, transforming societal needs into opportunities for sustainable enterprise. An illustrative case is that of a business that employs homeless individuals, thereby addressing a social issue while also creating economic value.

Wealth redistribution is perhaps the most contentious term we shall dissect, often evoking visceral reactions on all sides of the political spectrum. It refers to the transfer of wealth from the rich to the poor, ideally in a manner that promotes fairer access to opportunities and resources. It's a principle that can be seen in progressive taxation, where those with greater economic means contribute a larger share to the welfare of society.

Each of these terms, while distinct, weaves into the tapestry of moral economics, a concept that champions the welfare of humanity over the accumulation of capital. They are not esoteric jargon but practical ideals, rooted in the real struggles and aspirations of people across the world.

The tapestry of these concepts forms a mosaic that challenges the status quo, beckoning us toward a future where our economies serve not as engines of inequality but as instruments of harmony and human flourishing. As we delve into the substance of these ideas, let us hold fast to the vision of Diadidomi—a world where giving supersedes receiving, where the wealth of a few is not hoarded but shared for the benefit of all.

This exploration is not a mere academic exercise. It is an invitation to consider a different reality, to question the foundations of our current economic systems, and to dare to imagine a new paradigm. It is a journey into the heart of what it means to live not just for oneself but for the greater good.

In the chapters that follow, we will dissect these terms with the precision of a surgeon and the insight of a sage. We will weave together the threads of theory and practice, painting a picture of a world where moral economics is not a utopian fantasy but a lived reality. This is the path to a future where greed is not the ruler but the outcast, where the economy is a garden that nourishes all who dwell within it.

The road ahead is long, and the work to be done is immense. But the map is before us, the compass in our hands. Let us step forward with the courage of conviction and the strength of our shared humanity, guided by the principles of moral economics and the enduring wisdom of Diadidomi.

The Redistribution Revolution

As dawn broke over the cobblestone streets of Paris in 1789, the air was thick with the scent of change. The old regime, a symbol of opulence and oppression, stood on the brink of a revolution that would shake the very foundations of society. The common people, long burdened by the weight of inequality and injustice, were poised to reclaim their rights and reshape their destiny. This was a seminal moment in history, one that would echo through the ages and ignite a spark of hope for future generations.

The French Revolution was but one of many historical milestones that would pave the way for radical ideas like redistribution. From the overthrowing of monarchies to the rise of socialist states, the centuries that followed bore witness to a world in tumult, grappling with the distribution of wealth and power. The industrial revolution further accelerated economic disparities, creating a chasm between the burgeoning capitalist class and the toiling labor force.

Fast forward to the present, and the vestiges of these events are still palpably felt. The chasm has widened, and the call for redistribution has grown louder. In the shadows of towering skyscrapers, the plight of the working poor whispers a stark reminder of unresolved issues. While technological advancements have propelled some to unprecedented prosperity, others languish in the forgotten corners of society, where opportunity seems but a distant dream.

Why does this history matter now? It matters because the past holds lessons for the present, and the present is rife with opportunities to shape the future. Understanding the roots of wealth inequality is crucial in addressing the systematic imbalances that plague our current economic landscape. History is not just a record of what has been; it is a compass that can guide us toward a more just and equitable society.

Now, let us delve into the contemporary exploration of redistribution, a concept as old as civilization itself, yet as urgent as the morning headlines. Redistribution, or Diadidomi, is not a mere academic term—it is a call to action, a paradigm shift that can forge a path toward a society where the fruits of labor and the bounties of progress are shared more fairly among all.

Imagine, if you will, a world where the vast wealth of a nation is not hoarded by the few but is instead invested in the many. Picture a society where education, healthcare, and opportunity are accessible to all, not just the privileged. Can you see it? Do you dare to dream of it? This is the vision of the Redistribution Revolution.

But how does one go about creating such a society? The answer lies in the principles of Diadidomi, which advocate for a giving hand rather than a clenched fist. Redistribution is not about taking from the rich to give to the poor in perpetuity; it is about creating systems that naturally balance the scales of prosperity.

Let's take, for example, the concept of a guaranteed basic income—a bold idea that has gained traction in recent years. What if every citizen were assured a living wage, irrespective of their employment status? Such a system could potentially eradicate poverty, spur innovation, and unleash the full potential of the human spirit. It's an idea that challenges us to rethink the very nature of work and reward in society.

The Redistribution Revolution does not stop at financial measures. It encompasses access to quality education, to ensure that every child, regardless of their socioeconomic background, can dream big and achieve those dreams. It extends to healthcare, ensuring that no one is denied the right to wellness. It includes housing, so that every person has a place to call home, a sanctuary where they can thrive.

The road to a more egalitarian society is fraught with obstacles. There will be those who resist change, who cling to the antiquated notions of hierarchy and privilege. But the winds of change are relentless, and they whisper a simple truth: that a society that uplifts its weakest members stands strongest.

As we close this chapter and look toward the horizon, let us remember that the Redistribution Revolution is not just a distant hope—it is a living, breathing movement that begins with each of us. It is a collective journey toward a future where every human being is valued, where the measure of a society is not in its stockpiles of wealth but in the well-being of its people.

The Redistribution Revolution is about writing a new story for humanity—a story where compassion and equity are not just ideals but the cornerstones of our world. It is about creating a legacy that we can be proud to leave behind, a testament to the enduring power of giving and the unyielding spirit of progress.

Together, let us move forward, with the lessons of history as our guide and the promise of a better future as our motivation. This is our time, this is our cause, and this is our revolution—the Redistribution Revolution.

Generosity as Policy

In the ever-unfolding narrative of human progress, where do we find ourselves today? The question hangs in the air, poignant and heavy with implication. A world draped in technological marvels, yet still marred by the age-old blight of greed and disparity. It's a juxtaposition that begs for resolution, for a catalyst that will drive us toward a more harmonious existence. This catalyst, perhaps, may be found in a concept that is as timeless as humanity itself: generosity.

But what happens when generosity transcends the individual and becomes a blueprint for societal structure? When the act of giving is not merely recommended but woven into the very fabric of policy? This is where our journey into institutionalizing generosity begins.

The current issue is stark – economic inequality has reached unprecedented levels, and the divide continues to grow. The wealthiest individuals and corporations amass fortunes that are inconceivable to the average person, while many struggle to afford basic necessities. The repercussions of this imbalance are manifold: social unrest, health disparities, and stifled economic mobility are but a few of the troubling consequences.

If left unchecked, the chasm between the wealthy and the impoverished will only widen, leading to a frayed social fabric that could unravel the cohesion of entire communities. Imagine a world where access to life's essentials is so polarized that the concept of a middle class is rendered obsolete. The potential for conflict, both within and across borders, looms like storm clouds on the horizon.

So, what path can we take to avert such a grim future? The answer lies in policy changes inspired by Diadidomi – the spirit of sharing and giving. By embedding generosity into our institutions, we can build systems that inherently counteract greed.

A practical solution takes form in the proposal of a progressive tax system that ensures the wealthiest individuals and corporations contribute a fair share to the public coffers. This is not a punitive measure but a recalibration of responsibility to the society that has enabled their success. The revenue generated could fund social programs, education, and healthcare, setting the stage for a more equitable distribution of resources.

To implement such a policy, we must first foster broad public support. This involves educating the populace on the benefits of a more equitable tax structure, dispelling myths about its impact on economic growth, and showcasing examples where similar systems have been successful.

Looking at past outcomes, we find that countries with progressive taxation often experience higher levels of happiness and social well-being. Predictions for future outcomes suggest that, by reducing economic inequality, we can foster a more stable and productive society.

Another solution to consider is the introduction of laws that encourage corporate philanthropy and social responsibility. Imagine companies competing not just for profit, but for the positive impact they can make on their communities and the environment. The implementation of such laws would involve setting clear guidelines and incentives for businesses to invest in the public good.

There are, of course, alternative solutions. One could argue for a more laissez-faire approach, trusting that the invisible hand of the market will eventually address these disparities. Others might advocate for voluntary charity as a means to bridge the gap. While these options merit consideration, they lack the systematic approach necessary to address the scale of the problem at hand.

As you ponder these propositions, let the image of a society bound not by self-interest but by the collective pursuit of the greater good linger in your mind. Can we dare to dream of such a world?

Generosity as a policy is not a panacea, but it is a step toward a future where success is measured by more than personal accumulation. It is a world where the power of giving is recognized as the foundation for a thriving society.

Thus, we embark on this quest not blindly, but guided by the light of evidence and the compass of our shared humanity. It is an invitation to rewrite the story of our times, to sculpt a legacy that will echo through the annals of history, not as a whisper but as a resounding call to action. May we rise to the challenge, for the sake of all who will walk this earth after us.

Generosity as policy is more than an ideal; it is a beacon that illuminates the path to a world where every individual is empowered to live with dignity and opportunity. It is a journey we undertake together, with the wisdom of the past and the hope of the future as our steadfast allies.

Reshaping Hearts and Markets

In a world teetering on the brink of self-induced calamity, the question that ignites minds and stirs the soul is this: Can we sculpt a future that celebrates both the individual's heart and the collective pulse of the market? The Diadidomi principles offer a beacon of hope, a philosophy that could reshape the landscape of human interaction and economic exchange. Herein lies a sequential roadmap, a guide through the transformative power of Diadidomi—reshaping hearts and markets for the betterment of all.

The end in sight is clear: to weave the fabric of Diadidomi into the very essence of our society, creating a tapestry where every thread supports the other, where the warp of individual endeavor interlaces with the weft of collective welfare.

To embark on this ambitious journey, one must be armed with an understanding of Diadidomi, a willingness to embrace change, and the resolve to act. A broad overview points to education, policy reform, and cultural shift as the stepping stones toward our goal. The path ahead is neither simple nor straightforward, but the destination is worthy of the trek.

As we delve deeper, each step unfurls with greater clarity. Education, the cornerstone of transformation, must be re-envisioned to instill the values of Diadidomi from the earliest of years. Schools become incubators for generosity and empathy, fostering a new generation primed to carry the torch of change.

Moving to policy reform, we advocate for systems that incentivize giving and communal success. Tax incentives for charitable contributions, government support for social enterprises, and the establishment of 'giving floors'—minimum percentages of income dedicated to philanthropy—are just the beginning.

On the cultural front, we must champion the stories of those who live by Diadidomi. Every act of generosity, every company that prioritizes societal well-being, every policy that narrows the chasm of inequality—these are the narratives that must be amplified.

Heed these tips and warnings: Change is often met with resistance. The inertia of tradition and the stronghold of the status quo are formidable adversaries. Forewarned, we must persevere, knowing the fruits of Diadidomi are worth the struggle.

Testing the success of our endeavors is essential. We seek a reduction in economic disparities, a rise in philanthropic activities, and a palpable shift in societal values. Surveys, studies, and statistics will chart our progress, but the true measure of success lies in the lived experiences of the people.

Should we encounter setbacks, our troubleshooting must be as innovative as our vision. When policies falter, we iterate. When cultural shifts stall, we inspire anew. And when the heart of the individual seems unmoved by the plight of the many, we strive to touch that heart with stories that resonate.

Imagine, if you will, a marketplace where every exchange is infused with the spirit of Diadidomi. Where consumers and producers are partners in progress, where the success of one is not the downfall of another. This is the future we are crafting, one decision, one policy, one heart at a time.

Could it be that the solution to our most intractable problems lies not in more regulation, but in more compassion? Does the key to sustainable economies rest within the depths of human generosity? These are the questions we must dare to ask, and in the asking, we open the door to new possibilities.

Let us not rely solely on the written word to convey our message. Allow the voices of those transformed by Diadidomi to speak. "Before Diadidomi, I viewed success as a personal conquest," shares a once-avaricious CEO. "Now, I see that my true legacy is what I give, not what I take."

As the pages of this book turn, let us remember that each sentence is but a brushstroke in a larger painting. Our collective efforts create a masterpiece of a society that values the well-being of all. The journey of Diadidomi is one of continuous learning, unyielding commitment, and the unshakable belief that together, we can reshape hearts and markets for a future that shines with the promise of shared prosperity and enduring harmony.

So, we march forth, not as solitary warriors, but as a legion united by a common cause. The Diadidomi principles are our creed, our shared heartbeat that pumps vitality into the veins of the market. It's a symphony of actions and intentions, resonating with the rhythm of change.

In conclusion, may the spirit of Diadidomi guide your every step as you join us in this crusade against indifference and inequality. Together, let us build a world where the currency of generosity enriches us all, where markets serve not just the few, but the many. This is our quest, our noble pursuit—reshaping hearts and markets for a brighter tomorrow.

5

——————

FEEDING THE WORLD

The Hunger Paradox

In a world brimming with technological marvels and agricultural advancements, it is a confounding reality that millions still lay their heads down each night on an empty stomach. The Hunger Paradox, as it's commonly deemed, is not just a distant concept discussed at summits or a statistic that occasionally surfaces in the news. It's a daily, grinding reality for a substantial segment of humanity, one that exists alongside the contrasting abundance of food in other parts of the globe. This cruel irony is the crux of the matter at hand, one that Diadidomi—an innovative initiative dedicated to equitable food distribution—seeks to address.

The conundrum is stark: how can a planet that produces more than enough food to feed every soul be home to such widespread hunger? We produce enough calories, enough wheat, enough rice, and yet, gaping mouths and gnawing stomachs persist. This paradox is not merely a logistical nightmare; it is a moral quandary, challenging the very fabric of our global community. Through the narrative of Diadidomi, we embark on a journey to unravel this perplexing issue, seeking answers hidden within the labyrinth of global food politics, economic disparities, and the environmental crisis.

The impact of this paradox is not a mere ripple across the water, it's a tsunami that washes away lives, hopes, and futures. Imagine the potential of a child stunted, not by a lack of ambition, but by a lack of nutrition. Picture villages where the fields are fertile but the stomachs are perpetually hollow. This is the landscape of the hunger paradox—a place where plenty and want reside side by side, separated by invisible lines of inequity and indifference.

To personalize the issue, let us tell you about Amina, a young girl from a small farming community in Sub-Saharan Africa. Amina's days begin before the sun pierces the horizon, fetching water from a distant well. Her family's land, rich in soil, yields bountiful harvests of maize and beans. Yet, Amina's little brother's belly is distended, not from nourishment, but from malnutrition. The irony? The surplus from their harvest is sold for a pittance to middlemen who then export it to countries where food is wasted daily. Amina's story is one of countless others, a testament to the skewed scales of global food distribution.

The stakes could not be higher. When we consider the implications of the hunger paradox, we face the potential collapse of entire communities, the loss of generations, and the perpetuation of a cycle of poverty that grips the most vulnerable. This is no longer a distant problem; it is an imminent threat that requires immediate, unequivocal action.

As we delve into the following chapters, Diadidomi will offer a beacon of hope. We will explore innovative agricultural practices, delve into the intricacies of food trade policies, and highlight the transformative power of community-based initiatives. At the heart of Diadidomi's response is a commitment to not only feed the hungry but to empower individuals and communities to sustainably produce and access the food they need.

We will witness the power of partnerships that bridge the divide between excess and need, and we will meet the champions of change who are rewriting the narrative of hunger. From high-tech vertical farms in urban metropolises to the revival of ancient grains in rural heartlands, Diadidomi's story is one of resilience, creativity, and hope.

Have you ever considered the absurdity that in some corners of the world, supermarkets discard mountains of unsold produce while, in others, markets are bare? Diadidomi contemplates this, challenging us to rethink our relationship with food and our responsibility toward our fellow humans. Can we, as a collective, shift the paradigm from consumption to compassion, from waste to wisdom?

As you turn each page, you will uncover the layers that contribute to the hunger paradox. You will meet individuals who are transforming the lives of their communities one meal at a time. Each chapter is a step toward understanding, a guide to action, and a call to arms.

In the end, the Hunger Paradox is not merely a challenge to be solved; it is an opportunity to manifest the best of human ingenuity and empathy. It is a chance to reshape our world, to ensure that abundance is not a privilege but a right shared by all. Diadidomi's journey is not just about feeding the hungry; it's about nourishing the soul of humanity.

Are you ready to be part of the solution? Will you join us as we embark on this transformative journey? Let Diadidomi guide you through the complexities of the hunger paradox, toward a future where no child, no family, no community goes to bed hungry. Together, we can turn the paradox into a past memory, and the abundance into a shared reality for every person on this planet.

Diadidomi's Bread of Life

In the olive groves of ancient Greece, the idea of Diadidomi —giving through sharing—found its earliest expression. It was a time when philosophers contemplated the essence of life, and the common meal, or agape feast, symbolized the union of souls and the sharing of Earth's bounty. This ethos, deeply entwined with the concept of the 'Bread of Life,' has transcended ages, shaping the very foundation of how we perceive sustenance and community.

Throughout history, the 'Bread of Life' has been a powerful symbol. In the Judeo-Christian tradition, it represents provision and spiritual nourishment—man does not live by bread alone but thrives on every word that comes from the divine. In the times of the Roman Empire, the distribution of grain was not only a means of sustenance but also a method of control, 'panem et circenses' as the saying went—bread and circuses to appease the masses.

As centuries turned, the world saw empires rise and fall, each leaving their mark on how societies distributed and valued their food. The Middle Ages brought feudal systems where the serfs worked the land and the lords reaped the harvests, often leaving little for those who toiled. The Renaissance ushered in new thinking about humanism and individual worth, subtly altering the dynamics of food sharing and charity.

The Industrial Revolution was a catalyst for profound change. With urbanization, the intimate relationship between man and land was disrupted. Food became a commodity, and its distribution, a business. As populations swelled in the burgeoning cities, so did the gap between the haves and the have-nots. The 20th century, with its world wars and economic depressions, only exacerbated this divide, leading to unprecedented levels of hunger amid plenty.

Now, as we stand in the 21st century, the echoes of history ring loud. We face a modern world where the paradox of hunger amidst abundance persists. Yet, the age-old tradition of Diadidomi, the giving for the greater good, provides a beacon of hope.

Why does this historical journey matter today? Because to solve a problem as complex as hunger, we must understand its roots. The past illuminates the present, shedding light on the patterns of inequality and exploitation that have led us here. It is only by acknowledging these truths that we can move forward with solutions that are just and sustainable.

The story of Diadidomi's Bread of Life is not a mere recounting of the past. It is a call to action, a charge to take up the baton of those who have gone before us in the fight against hunger. Consider the power of a single loaf of bread. It can be broken into many pieces, shared among many mouths, and in its division, it multiplies. It becomes more than food; it becomes a testament to our shared humanity. Do we not owe it to each other to ensure that no person goes without this basic sustenance?

As we delve deeper into the narrative, we will explore the innovative and transformative initiatives that are breathing new life into the ancient tradition of Diadidomi. From the community gardens sprouting in urban food deserts to the global movements advocating for food sovereignty, these are the modern-day loaves and fish stories.

Have you ever wondered what it would take to nourish not just the body, but the spirit of our global village? Can we rekindle the communal fires of the agape feast in this digital age? These are the questions that Diadidomi's Bread of Life invites you to ponder.

Imagine a world where food is not a weapon of power but a bridge to peace. Envision communities where the abundance of some does not spell scarcity for others. This is the world that Diadidomi aspires to create—one where the Bread of Life is available to all, nourishing, sustaining, and uniting us in our shared humanity.

As we break the bread of knowledge and share its crumbs through these pages, let us remember that the essence of Diadidomi is not only about giving but also about receiving with grace. For in the act of accepting, we acknowledge our interconnectedness and the cyclical nature of life's gifts.

You are now part of this age-old yet ever-new story of Diadidomi. Together, let us rise to the challenge and ensure that the Bread of Life is not a luxury, but a basic right that binds us all in dignity and respect.

Will you join us in this mission? Will you be the hand that both gives and receives, the voice that speaks up for the silent? Let us embark on this transformative journey with Diadidomi, and let the Bread of Life be the sustenance that propels us toward a future where hunger is but a distant memory.

Agricultural Generosity

In the fertile heartland of a developing nation, where the sun bathes the earth in a warm, golden glow, a small community sets the stage for a remarkable transformation. Fields stretch out like a checkerboard of varying hues of green and gold, interrupted only by the occasional tree or winding dirt road. Here, the earth is both the canvas and the medium for an age-old art: agriculture.

Our main players in this unfolding narrative are a collective of local farmers, an agricultural scientist named Dr. Maria Gomez, and a non-profit organization called "Harvest of Hope." The farmers, with hands as weathered as the soil they till, are the unsung heroes of this tale—custodians of the land and the knowledge that comes from generations of toiling upon it. Dr. Gomez, with her deep understanding of agronomy and a heart for the people, bridges the gap between traditional wisdom and modern science. "Harvest of Hope" serves as a conduit for change, providing resources and support to fuel the community's journey toward sustainable abundance.

The challenge that brought them together was as old as agriculture itself yet amplified by contemporary issues: food insecurity. Despite their relentless labor, the farmers' yields were inconsistent, often failing to meet the needs of their community, let alone allowing for surplus to share or sell. Unpredictable weather patterns, a consequence of climate change, and the lack of access to modern techniques compounded their struggles.

Dr. Gomez introduced the concept of Diadidomi-inspired agricultural practices, rooted in the principle of generosity and sustainability. She worked alongside the farmers, integrating their knowledge with innovations such as crop rotation, organic pest control, and water conservation techniques. "Harvest of Hope" supported the initiative by funding necessary tools and training, turning the soil of cooperation into a bedrock for growth.

The results, harvested over several seasons, were nothing short of miraculous. Crop yields increased by an impressive 70%, with a substantial decrease in loss due to pests or disease. The community's food security improved, and the surplus produce found its way to local markets, invigorating the local economy and fostering a spirit of abundance.

But the triumphs were not solely measured in bushels and currency. The rejuvenated spirit of the community, the smiles on the children's faces as they bit into fresh fruit, and the renewed sense of hope were the true yields of this endeavor. Reflections on the journey revealed important lessons: that marrying innovation with tradition could yield astonishing results, and that the heart of sustainability lies in the willingness to share knowledge and resources.

Visual aids punctuated the narrative at seminars and workshops hosted by "Harvest of Hope," illustrating the stark contrast between the withered fields of yesterday and the lush crops of today. Charts and graphs underscored the tangible benefits, but it was the photographs of the community, vibrant and thriving, that truly captured the essence of the transformation.

This specific instance, though small on the grand scale of global agriculture, serves as a microcosm of what is possible when the principles of Diadidomi inform our practices. It is a testament to the fact that when we give generously—be it knowledge, resources, or time—the returns can extend far beyond what we might anticipate.

As we ponder this case study, a question lingers in the air, ripe as the fruit in those rejuvenated fields: If such a transformation is possible in a single community, what could we achieve on a global scale if the ethos of Diadidomi were woven into the fabric of our agricultural systems?

As I, Kirk Anthony, reflect upon my life's journey—from a nine-year-old child graced by divine revelation to a decorated Air Force veteran and scholar of econometrics—I see the threads of Diadidomi woven throughout. Each milestone, each accolade, is a reminder of the potency of sharing, of the multiplicative power of giving.

Now, through the pages of this book and the seeds of thought it plants, I invite you to join the revolution of Agricultural Generosity. To embrace the call to nurture not just the soil beneath our feet, but the very soul of our global community. For in the end, the true harvest lies in the hearts we touch and the lives we lift.

And so, dear reader, as we turn the page on this chapter, let us carry with us the spirit of Diadidomi. May it guide our hands as we till the fields of change, and may the Bread of Life grow ever more abundant in the shared garden of our collective future.

Community-Based Solutions

Dawn had barely broken when Miguel's boots hit the dew-kissed earth of his ancestors' land. A stubborn mist clung to the rows of burgeoning crops, and the roosters heralded the day with their unabashed crowing. In the small village of Esperanza, the people held a simple truth close to their hearts: the land was a living, breathing entity, and they were its humble caretakers.

Miguel, a third-generation farmer with skin bronzed by the sun and eyes that mirrored the depth of the earth, was a protagonist in a story of resilience. His calloused hands were a testament to years of battling the whims of nature to provide for his family and community. He was the embodiment of Diadidomi, though he'd never heard the term. For him, the act of giving was as natural as the cycles of the seasons.

On this particular morning, Miguel's journey took an unexpected detour. He discovered a group of young volunteers, led by a sprightly woman known to the village as "Sister Ana," planting trees at the periphery of his field. Sister Ana, a retired schoolteacher and a firm believer in grassroots activism, had a vision to combat soil erosion and create a microclimate beneficial to the crops.

Miguel watched, intrigued as the volunteers worked with a rhythm that spoke of unity and purpose. They were not merely planting trees; they were sowing seeds of hope, interlacing their roots with the soil of community and the promise of sustainable life. As Sister Ana caught Miguel's eye, she beckoned him over, her eyes alight with an unspoken invitation to join the unexpected journey.

"My friends," Sister Ana addressed the group, pausing to wipe her brow, "this man is not just a farmer. He is the steward of our shared future. Miguel, we plant these trees for you, for us, and for the generations to come. Will you help us?"

Might this simple act of planting trees be a microcosm of a greater truth? That each of us holds the power to instigate change, to contribute to a collective well-being that transcends our individual lives? This was the universal thread Miguel felt tug at his soul, resonating with a wisdom that was both ancient and urgently relevant.

As he knelt beside Sister Ana, accepting the sapling she offered, Miguel realized that this was more than cooperation; it was communion. Here, in the shared labor of their hands, lay the valuable insights and revelations that promised a richer harvest than any single crop could yield.

Throughout the pages that follow, you, the reader, will be invited to witness and partake in the stories of communities like Esperanza. Each tale is a mosaic piece in the grand design of food security, framed by the spirit of Diadidomi.

We'll venture into urban gardens nestled between the cold concrete of cityscapes, where community leaders transform vacant lots into verdant oases. We'll visit schools where children learn the alchemy of turning seeds into sustenance, their laughter rising like the sprouts they tend.

Can you imagine a world where such initiatives are the norm rather than the exception? Where the knowledge of food production is as fundamental as reading and writing? I dare you to envision it. And then, I urge you to act upon that vision.

Our collective journey is marked by the milestones of the ordinary folks who choose to act extraordinarily. They do not seek fame or fortune but operate under the ethos that to live is to give, and to give is to thrive.

As Kirk Anthony, I have witnessed the power of Diadidomi firsthand, both in spiritual and secular arenas. My life's tapestry, woven with the threads of academic achievement and spiritual pursuit, has led me to a profound understanding: the solutions we seek for global challenges often sprout from the fertile ground of local action.

Dear reader, as you delve deeper into "Community-Based Solutions," let the stories of these unsung heroes inspire you. May their commitment to Diadidomi ignite a flame within your heart—a flame that warms, illuminates, and most importantly, spreads.

It is in the sharing of our stories, our successes, and our setbacks that we discover the strength to nurture the garden of humanity. It is here, in the communion of shared purpose, that we find the true essence of food security—a security that feeds not just the body but also the soul.

And so, let us walk together through the ensuing chapters, each step a testament to the enduring spirit of community and the transformative power of Diadidomi. May we emerge from this journey not just informed, but transformed, ready to plant our own trees of hope in the ever-growing forest of human endeavor.

Policy Proposals for Hunger Eradication

In the tapestry of human existence, hunger remains one of the most profound and pervasive threads, woven deeply into the fabric of societies. Despite the strides made in technology and agriculture, the specter of hunger still looms large over millions, casting a long shadow on our collective conscience. Why, in a world brimming with abundance, must empty bellies and malnourished children persist?

The hunger crisis is a multifaceted specter, a hydra-headed challenge that ensnares nations in a cycle of poverty, disease, and despair. It is a silent tsunami that sweeps away the potential of generations, leaving in its wake societies that are fragile and stunted. But what if this cycle could be broken? What if the principles of Diadidomi, the very essence of giving and sharing, could be the key to unlocking a future free from the shackles of hunger?

Picture, if you will, a world where every child has the nourishment needed to grow, learn, and thrive. A world where farmers, like Miguel, are not only custodians of the land but also guardians of their community's well-being. This is not a utopian fantasy; it is a tangible reality that can be achieved through deliberate, compassionate policy-making.

First, we must identify the roots of hunger with unflinching clarity. The issue is not merely a lack of food but a deficiency in access, distribution, and equity. Food waste, economic disparity, and political instability all contribute to the hunger crisis. How can it be that supermarkets dispose of mountains of edible food while stomachs rumble in the shadows of those very buildings?

The consequences of inaction are dire and far-reaching. Malnutrition cripples the immune system, leaving the body vulnerable to diseases that would otherwise be mere nuisances. It stifles cognitive development in children, robbing them of the chance to achieve their full intellectual potential. Economies suffer as a malnourished workforce lacks the vitality to drive progress. The fabric of society unravels when its members cannot meet their most basic needs.

But despair not, for there are solutions at hand—solutions steeped in the Diadidomi philosophy. Imagine policies that incentivize the reduction of food waste, transforming excess into hope for those in need. Envision agricultural subsidies not just for large agribusinesses, but for smallholders who practice sustainable farming, ensuring that they can continue to nourish their communities.

And what of the implementation? It begins with collaboration—governments, NGOs, and the private sector, all converging with a singular aim: to eradicate hunger. Such policies could include creating food recovery networks, bolstering local food systems, and investing in infrastructure that connects producers directly with consumers, cutting out the wasteful middlemen.

Evidence of success is not scarce. Look to the initiatives that have turned barren urban landscapes into productive community gardens. Observe the school feeding programs that have boosted attendance and academic performance by providing students with a reliable source of nutrition. These are but glimpses of what can be achieved when policy is infused with compassion and foresight.

Are there alternative solutions? Certainly. Some advocate for technological innovations like genetically modified crops to increase yield, while others propose a universal basic income to address poverty at its core. Yet, these too must be approached with the spirit of Diadidomi, ensuring that they serve the many rather than the few.

And so, we stand at a crossroads. Will we choose the path of apathy, or will we embrace the principles of Diadidomi to forge a world where hunger is but a memory? The answer lies not only in the halls of power but also in the fields, the classrooms, and the community centers where the true heartbeat of change resonates.

Let us rally behind the policy proposals that can turn the tide against hunger. Let us commit to a future where the earth's bounty is shared equitably, and every human being can partake in the harvest. This is no mere dream; it is a call to action—a call that echoes the timeless truth that to live is to give, and to give is to truly live.

We have the tools. We have the knowledge. Now, all we need is the collective will to make Diadidomi not just a word, but a way of life. Can we rise to this challenge? The answer, resoundingly, must be 'yes.'

6

THE DEATH OF DEATH

Understanding 'The Last Enemy'

In the hushed sanctuaries of the heart, where the soul wrestles with the profound and the eternal, there often lingers a shadow that is as old as humanity itself. It is a presence that whispers of finality, a specter that looms at the conclusion of every life's narrative. This presence, this specter, is what the Christian tradition has named 'The Last Enemy.' But what is the nature of this adversary? How does Diadidomi, the act of giving through and beyond oneself, engage with this formidable foe?

'The Last Enemy' is not a foe of flesh and blood, nor is it a conquerable territory. It is death itself. In Christian thought, death is seen not merely as a natural process but as an intruder, an aberration birthed from mankind's primordial rebellion against the divine. It is the cessation of life, the thief of breath and being—the ultimate separation of the soul from both body and Creator.

To elaborate, this 'enemy' is framed within the narrative of salvation history. It is the final hurdle before the consummation of all things, where the Christian hope professes that death will be swallowed up in victory. It is the last note of discord in a symphony that shall eventually resolve into perfect harmony.

The etymology of 'enemy' stems from the Latin 'inimicus,' meaning 'not a friend.' Over time, the word has come to signify any force or entity that is antagonistic to one's well-being. When applied to death, it becomes a metaphor for the ultimate opposition to life and to the Christian promise of eternal fellowship with God.

Diadidomi then, as a theological concept, is situated within this grander narrative—a countermeasure to 'The Last Enemy.' It entails a sacrificial giving, a sharing, and a passing on of oneself for the sake of others. In essence, it is the antithesis of the isolating and consuming nature of death.

In the real world, Diadidomi confronts the last enemy in acts of selfless love and in the hope of resurrection. It is seen in the care for the dying, in the comfort for the grieving, and in the Christian community's defiant proclamation that death does not have the final word. Stories abound of individuals who, even on their deathbeds, manifest this giving spirit—

offering forgiveness, imparting wisdom, and bequeathing a legacy of faith.

Yet, there are misconceptions that must be dispelled. Some view death as a friend, a release from suffering, or even as the ultimate end. While these notions might provide temporary solace, they do not align with the Christian understanding of death as an enemy, nor do they acknowledge the full scope of Diadidomi's transformative power.

Does this understanding not stir within you a sense of urgency? A call to live with purpose, knowing that each moment is a precious gift to be given away in love? Can you feel the weight of eternity pressing upon the temporal, urging a life of Diadidomi that defies the shadow of 'The Last Enemy'?

Our language, too, must be refined. Let us not speak of death with frivolity or fatalism. Instead, let our words be imbued with the resolve of hope. For in the Christian worldview, death's sting is ultimately dulled by the resurrection, its victory undone by the empty tomb.

But still, one might ask, how can something as paradoxical as giving oneself away defeat something as final as death? It is in the rhythm of sacrificial love, in the cadence of self-giving that echoes the divine, where we find our answer. It is in the Christ-like surrender, where one's life becomes a gift for many, that death's grip is loosened.

Consider the whisper of a mother to her child, the last

breath of a saint, the final stroke of a painter's brush—all Diadidomi, all testimonies that life, given away in love, transcends the grave.

In conclusion, 'The Last Enemy' is not a concept to be feared but engaged with through the theology and practice of Diadidomi. By understanding death from this perspective, Christians are called to live lives of profound generosity, where the act of giving becomes a proclamation of hope and a witness to the resurrection. It is in this giving that we find the truest form of living, a life that defies death and echoes into eternity.

So let us embrace Diadidomi with fervor, for in doing so, we affirm that love is stronger than death, and in the economy of the divine, the last enemy to be destroyed is death itself.

Diadidomi and Health Economics

In the expansive domain of human inquiry, where intellect and emotion interlace, there emerges a profound intersection between the philosophical and the practical. This juncture is where the ancient art of Diadidomi meets the modern science of health economics—a discipline concerned with the optimization of health and wellness through the allocation of resources. At the heart of this exploration lies a fundamental question: Can Diadidomi, the selfless act of giving, catalyze a transformative impact on the economics of health?

Universal wellness, an ideal in which every individual has access to the necessary means to achieve their optimal state of health, is a vision as alluring as it is elusive. But what if this vision could be brought closer to reality through the principles of Diadidomi? What if the key to unlocking this potential lies in the very fabric of human generosity and interconnectedness?

To dissect this proposition, we delve into the primary evidence—the tangible effects of Diadidomi on health outcomes. Studies indicate that altruism can lead to significant improvements in mental health, with donors often experiencing a 'helper's high,' a state of euphoria linked to the release of endorphins. Further, the act of giving has been associated with lower blood pressure, reduced stress levels, and even increased longevity. These findings suggest that Diadidomi is not merely a lofty ideal but a practical pathway to individual well-being.

But let us venture deeper into the evidence. The implications of Diadidomi extend beyond individual health gains to encompass systemic benefits. For instance, voluntary blood donations embody Diadidomi and are critical to saving lives, reducing the economic burden of blood procurement, and enhancing the efficiency of healthcare systems. Similarly, organ donations alleviate the need for expensive long-term treatments, such as dialysis for kidney failure patients, thereby freeing up resources for other healthcare needs.

However, the narrative of Diadidomi in health economics is

not without its counter-evidence. Critics argue that reliance on altruism for health resources could lead to unpredictability and inequality. They contend that voluntary giving may not be sufficient to meet the vast needs of healthcare systems, especially in times of crisis or in areas with lower socioeconomic status. This viewpoint challenges the initial claim by highlighting potential limitations in the scalability and sustainability of Diadidomi-based models.

In response to such critiques, it is essential to clarify that Diadidomi does not advocate for a wholesale replacement of established healthcare economics but rather seeks to complement and enhance it. The integration of altruistic practices within the framework of existing health policies can create synergies, where structured programs and incentives coexist with voluntary giving, ensuring a more robust and resilient system.

Let us not overlook additional evidence supporting the role of Diadidomi in health economics. Emerging models of community-based health insurance schemes, for example, are founded on principles of mutual aid and collective responsibility. These schemes demonstrate that communities can pool resources and share risks, leading to improved access to healthcare services for their members, especially in low-income settings.

As we draw this discourse to a close, we are compelled to reinforce the assertion that Diadidomi harbors the potential to significantly shape the landscape of health economics. By fostering a culture of giving and solidarity, we can pave the way for more inclusive, efficient, and compassionate health-care systems. The integration of Diadidomi into health economics does not offer a panacea; rather, it presents a beacon of hope—a testament to the power of human generosity in advancing the quest for universal wellness.

In considering the possibilities before us, one might ponder: How might our societies transform if the ethos of Diadidomi was woven into the very fabric of our healthcare systems? Could this integration be the dawn of a new era in health economics, an era characterized by a convergence of empathy and pragmatism?

In a world often marred by division and scarcity, the practice of Diadidomi stands as a reminder of our shared humanity and the boundless potential that arises when we give not just of our resources, but of ourselves. It challenges us to reimagine the dynamics of health economics, to envision a future where the act of giving becomes a cornerstone of universal wellness. Through this lens, we come to understand that the true wealth of a society may indeed be measured by the health and well-being of its members, and that perhaps, in the art of giving, we find the greatest gift of all.

Reimagining Mortality

Imagine a world where the boundaries of life are not dictated by the ticking clock of age, but by the depth of our generosity. This is no mere daydream; it is a promise, a gateway to a realm where the sands of time slow to a crawl, and the sun of vitality shines with unrelenting vigor. The principles of Diadidomi, when fully embraced, have the power to unfurl a tapestry of life that is both rich in years and quality. As you turn each page of "Reimagining Mortality," you stand on the precipice of understanding how a life led by selfless giving can extend your own existence in ways science is only beginning to understand.

The heart of Diadidomi beats with the rhythm of generosity, each pulse echoing through the corridors of our biological being. The evidence is irrefutable: those who give the experience a symphony of health benefits, from the harmonious balance of their mental state to the fortification of their physical health. But how can such a simple act, one that requires us to look beyond the confines of our own needs, catalyze such a profound effect on our longevity?

Skeptics may argue that the correlation between giving and longevity is a mere coincidence, a placebo effect dressed in the guise of medical fact. Yet, as we delve deeper into the science behind Diadidomi, the causal links become apparent, painting a clear picture that can no longer be dismissed as mere happenstance. The mechanisms at play are intricate, weaving through the fabric of our biological makeup, reinforcing our defenses, and rejuvenating our cells.

Envision, if you will, a journey where each step taken in the service of others not only lightens their burden but also strengthens your own vitality. Picture a life where the warmth of altruism thaws the ice of personal ailments, where the act of giving becomes a healing balm for both the giver and the receiver. This is the metamorphosis that offers —a transformation grounded not in wishful thinking, but in actionable principles that stand at the vanguard of extending human life.

Your commitment to exploring the vistas of this book is not merely an investment in knowledge; it is an affirmation of your desire to lead a life punctuated by meaning and profound longevity. The Diadidomi principles are not esoteric secrets, but accessible truths, ready to be woven into the fabric of your daily existence. Embrace them, and you embrace a future where aging is not feared but celebrated as a testament to a life generously lived.

As Kirk Anthony, my life's journey – from the divine revelation at nine, through the honor-laden halls of academia, to the founding of a spiritual college – has been a testament to the power of giving. The scholastic achievements and military decorations pale in comparison to the enlightenment gleaned from a life dedicated to Diadidomi. The econometric models taught and practiced in my college have revealed that the true measure of wealth is not in the accumulation but in the distribution of resources for the betterment of all.

You may ask, "Can I truly make a difference?" The answer resounds with a clarity that pierces through the cacophony of doubt. Yes, you can. Each act of kindness, each offering of time or resource, is a drop of vitality in the vast ocean of humanity. Together, these drops create a current strong enough to redefine the very essence of mortality.

Adverbs and adjectives, those enticing embellishments of language, find themselves sparse in this discourse. Instead, the verbs – give, heal, extend – serve as the robust pillars upon which the argument stands. They are the harbingers of action, the summoners of change.

Let us not forget the rhythm and cadence of our shared human experience, the ebb and flow of giving and receiving that dances through the pages of this work. It is a rhythm that beats stronger with each act of generosity, a cadence that sings the possibility of a new dawn for human health and longevity.

As you continue this journey through "Reimagining Mortality," allow the following words to echo in the chambers of your heart: "In giving, we receive; in bestowing, we are bestowed upon; and in extending the lives of others, we invariably extend our own." Through the lens of Diadidomi, every breath becomes a gift, every moment an opportunity, and every life a legacy of enduring vitality. Welcome to a world reimagined, where mortality is not a destination, but a path illuminated by the light of our own generosity.

Spiritual and Physical Longevity

In the realm of Diadidomi, the principles that govern spiritual benevolence intertwine gracefully with the tenets of physical wellness, each enhancing the other in a synergistic dance of well-being. This nexus of the ethereal and the corporeal forms the crux of "Spiritual and Physical Longevity," a journey that delves into the heart of how altruistic living not only enriches the soul but also fortifies the body.

This exploration is not an academic exercise; it is a quest for understanding the profound connections that unite the spiritual act of giving with the tangible outcome of enduring health. One may ponder the purpose behind such an investigation. It is, in essence, to uncover the veiled intricacies that allow the spirit's generosity to manifest as the body's resilience, offering us a blueprint for a life that transcends the ordinary limits of time and vitality.

To dissect this correlation meaningfully, we must establish a set of criteria, and benchmarks that allow us to measure the interplay between spiritual practice and physical longevity. Such metrics include the impact of stress reduction, the enhancement of immune function, and the promotion of psychological well-being—all facets of health touched by the spirit of Diadidomi.

When we place these subjects side by side, their similarities become strikingly clear. The peace that comes from a generous heart mirrors the tranquility that the body needs to repair and rejuvenate. Stress, a known accelerant of aging, seems to dissipate in the face of charitable actions, as if the act of giving casts a protective aura around the giver. This is not mere conjecture, for studies have shown that those who volunteer, who give of themselves to others, exhibit lower stress levels and, consequently, a reduced risk of chronic diseases.

Yet, as we juxtapose these elements, the contrasts are as enlightening as the parallels. The spiritual journey of Diadidomi is often intangible, its rewards felt within the depths of the soul. Physical longevity, on the other hand, is quantifiable, its markers etched in the biological reality of our bodies. Where giving is an act of faith, health is an outcome of fact. But the distinction does not diminish the connection; rather, it highlights the miraculous bridge that links the seen with the unseen.

Consider, for a moment, the visual aid of a tree. Its roots, buried deep within the earth, unseen, symbolize the spiritual principles of Diadidomi. The branches and leaves, visible and tangible, represent physical health. Just as the roots nourish the tree and enable its growth, so too does the spiritual nourish the physical, enabling a life of longevity.

The insights gleaned from this analysis are profound. They suggest that the pursuit of spiritual fulfillment through giving is not a solitary venture but one that carries with it the reward of physical vitality. It implies that our well-being is not compartmentalized into the spiritual or physical but is, instead, a holistic amalgamation of both.

We must then ask ourselves, how do these historical and theoretical comparisons translate into the contemporary landscape? In today's fast-paced, often materialistic world, the principles of Diadidomi stand as a bastion against the erosion of community and the decline of personal health. They serve as a reminder that in the act of reaching out to others, we inadvertently support the very foundations of our own well-being.

The details are intricate, the connections, complex. Yet, the language in which this story is told remains simple and accessible to all who seek its wisdom. It is a tale punctuated by the rhythm of giving, a cadence that resonates with the heartbeat of humanity. It is a narrative that unfolds through the actions of individuals, each contributing to the collective saga of our species' quest for longevity.

As we move forward, let us not forget the power of a single act of kindness, a solitary moment of generosity. It is in these seemingly small gestures that the seeds of spiritual and physical longevity are sown. In the end, as we extend our hands to others, we are also reaching out to our future selves, crafting a legacy of health and harmony that can stand the test of time.

Victory Over the Grave

The pall of the night had scarcely lifted when the distant hum of the city began to stir, a prelude to the dawn chorus of human hustle. Within this awakening sprawl lay a small, inconspicuous neighborhood, where the streets, etched with the wisdom of time, bore witness to the lives that tread upon them. It was here, in the embrace of these well-worn paths, that an extraordinary tale of resurgence was about to unfold.

Mariana, a woman with hair the color of twilight and eyes that held a reservoir of silent strength, was the unwitting protagonist of this morning's narrative. She lived in a modest house, one that hummed with the echoes of laughter and sorrow in equal measure. Her life, a tapestry of trials and triumphs, was a testament to the human spirit's resilience.

As the sun peeked over the horizon, painting the sky with shades of hope, Mariana faced yet another day in the battle against an illness that sought to claim her very essence. The prognosis had been grim, the options few, but within her chest beat the heart of a lioness, unyielding and fierce.

Each day was a delicate dance between hope and despair, a balance only those who have skirted the edges of mortality could truly comprehend. And yet, in the quiet moments of solitude, Mariana wove a defiant dream—one of victory, not over life, but over the specter of death that loomed ever close.

It was during one such morning, as the first light of dawn tickled the edges of her consciousness, that Mariana felt an unfamiliar sense of peace. In the absence of fear, a thought blossomed—could this be the day that the tide would turn? With this newfound resolve, she prepared to visit the community center, a haven that had become her sanctuary and the stage for her unexpected journey.

The center was a microcosm of Diadidomi, the very embodiment of mutual giving and receiving that had come to define Mariana's existence. Here, amidst the vibrant mélange of cultures and stories, she found solace and purpose, offering her own narrative as a beacon to others navigating the murky waters of adversity.

Mariana's story was not merely her own; it was a chapter in a larger chronicle of human endeavor. Each individual she met, and each life she touched, became threads in a rich tapestry, interwoven with the universal truths of struggle and redemption.

"My friends," Mariana would often begin, her voice a gentle caress against the backdrop of shared understanding, "we are more than the sum of our fears. We are the architects of our own destinies, builders of bridges over the chasms that life creates."

In the rapt attention of her audience lay the promise of wisdom, the anticipation of insights forged in the crucible of personal experience. Mariana's anecdote was but a gateway, opening onto a vista of profound understanding that each person could explore.

The stories shared within the walls of the community center transcended the individual, touching upon the eternal dance of life and death. They were narratives of courage, of ordinary people who, when faced with the abyss, chose to construct ladders to the stars instead of succumbing to the void.

How does one measure the impact of a life? Is it by the breaths we take, or the moments that take our breath away? Mariana's journey, steeped in the ethos of Diadidomi, suggested an answer that resonated with the pulse of humanity. It was in the giving that we receive; in the sharing of our burdens, we lighten our own load.

Mariana's victories were not solely her own; they belonged to the community that rallied around her, to every soul that found strength in her resilience. Her triumphs were a clarion call, echoing the potential within each person to rise above their circumstances, to claim victory over the grave—not through the avoidance of death, but through the embrace of life in all its fullness.

This is not a mere collection of stories; it is a tribute to the indomitable spirit that dwells within us all. It is a recognition that, even in the face of the most deathly circumstances, there lies the potential for renewal, for a resurgence that defies the finality of the grave.

As you journey through these pages, dear reader, may you find within them the echoes of your own story, the whispers of your own potential victory. And in the sharing of these narratives, may you discover the timeless wisdom that in the act of giving, in Diadidomi, we find the keys to unlock the chains that bind us to despair, paving the way to a life of boundless possibility.

Kirk Anthony, with the wisdom gleaned from a life dedicated to spiritual and scholastic pursuits, invites you to partake in the victory that awaits. For it is within these stories, these fragments of human endeavor, that we find the true measure of our own humanity.

7

THE WEALTH OF SALVATION

Salvation's Economic Dimensions

In the labyrinth of human existence, the quest for salvation often traverses the spiritual realm and overlooks the tangible corridors of the economic. Yet, in the discourse of liberation, the omission of economic prosperity is akin to a symphony without bass—the melody may soar, but the depth remains unexplored. To fully embrace the term 'salvation,' one must acknowledge its multifaceted nature, extending beyond the physical to nestle firmly in the financial realities that govern our world.

Understanding the intersection of salvation and economics requires a lexicon that bridges the divine and the material, the celestial and the commercial. Such an understanding is not merely an academic exercise; it is a critical component of comprehending the full scope of human liberation.

Embark, then, on a lexical journey through the terms that underpin this intersection: salvation, economics, liberation, and prosperity. In isolating these terms, we pave the way for a nuanced exploration of their collective significance.

The cornerstone of spiritual dialogue traditionally refers to the deliverance from sin and its consequences. It is often associated with the eternal soul's journey and the afterlife. However, when salvation's definition is expanded to include deliverance from the shackles of economic despair, it assumes a new urgent dimension.

The social science concerned with the production, distribution, and consumption of goods and services is the bedrock of societies. It is the engine that drives the prosperity of nations and individuals alike. When intertwined with salvation, economics becomes not just a matter of wealth, but a vital component of societal well-being.

Salvation implies a release from bondage or oppression, traditionally envisioned in a political or spiritual sense. However, economic liberation—the emancipation from poverty, inequality, and financial dependency—is a transformative concept that can reshape an individual's trajectory or the fate of an entire community.

Prosperity signifies more than mere affluence; it is the flourishing of human potential, the fruit of labor and ingenuity. When prosperity is viewed through the lens of salvation, it becomes a measure of the quality of life and the ability to fulfill one's purpose without the constraints of economic hardship.

Imagine, for a moment, a farmer in a fertile valley—a paragon of prosperity. The sun dapples through a canopy of green, kissing the earth below where seeds are cradled in the soil's embrace. Here, the term 'prosperity' is not an abstract concept. It is the yield of the harvest, the grain in the silo, the market's bustle where the fruits of labor are exchanged for currency—the currency that ensures the farmer's family thrives.

Each term, while distinct, is connected; they are strands woven into the fabric of an economically salvific narrative. Salvation in its expanded sense can no longer be confined to theological bounds. It reaches out, encompassing the well-being that comes with economic stability.

Ponder this: What is the value of a soul's salvation if the body it inhabits is ensnared by the chains of poverty? Can one truly experience spiritual deliverance while mired in financial ruin? Questions such as these challenge the traditional parameters of salvation and invite a deeper contemplation of its scope.

In the realm of economics, consider an individual's quest for liberation as they navigate a labyrinth of financial constraints. Their journey is not unlike that of a hero in an epic saga, where each decision can lead to prosperity or peril. The narrative of economic salvation is not a tale spun from fiction; it is the lived experience of countless individuals striving toward a future where financial stability is the cornerstone of their salvation.

Let us then delve into the complexities of economic salvation. Imagine a world where the pursuit of prosperity is not a Sisyphean task but a journey marked by milestones of achievement. Envision communities where the chains of fiscal oppression have been shattered, and liberation is not a distant dream but an attainable reality.

As our exploration concludes, we stand at the precipice of understanding, peering into the depths of salvation's economic dimensions. This is a realm where the spiritual and the material converge, where the pursuit of economic well-being is seen not as a divergence from the path of righteousness but as an integral part of the journey toward holistic salvation.

Prosperity With a Purpose

In a world ever teeming with aspirations and desires, the quest for prosperity often ascends to the summit of individual and collective goals. Yet, this pursuit, if hollow of purpose, can become a relentless chase where satisfaction remains as elusive as a mirage in a vast desert. What then does it mean to prosper with purpose, and how does this align with the ancient principle of Diadidomi, embodying the essence of giving and receiving in harmony with divine intention?

As dawn's light breaks over the horizon, casting golden hues across the awakening city, a significant challenge stirs beneath the bustle of progress. It is the challenge of inequality, the chasm between wealth and want, a social divide that threatens the very fabric of our communities. In this modern age, the disparity grows, painting a stark portrait of a society at odds with the notion of collective prosperity.

This imbalance presents a grim tableau; where excess and deprivation lie in uncomfortable proximity. The consequences of ignoring this problem are dire—social unrest, increased crime rates, and a declining sense of community. If left unaddressed, the very stability of our social structures is at stake, leading to a future where the divide is not merely economic but severs the heart of human connection.

Yet, there is a beacon of hope, a solution that can bridge this gap and create a paradigm of prosperity that serves all. This solution is rooted in the principle of Diadidomi—giving as one receives, a cycle of generosity that fosters a sense of unity and shared success. It is a call to weave purpose into the fabric of wealth creation, aligning material gain with the greater good.

Implementing this solution requires a shift in mindset, from individualism to collective well-being. It means businesses adopting practices that not only seek profit but also contribute to the community. It involves governments crafting policies that ensure economic growth is inclusive and benefits all strata of society. It requires individuals to cultivate a spirit of philanthropy, understanding that true prosperity comes from the enrichment of one's community, not just oneself.

Evidence of this principle's efficacy can be found in communities where cooperative models of business have thrived, where the wealth generated is reinvested into local initiatives, education, and healthcare—producing not only financial returns but social dividends as well. Predicted outcomes suggest that as more entities adopt this mindset, the cycle of giving and receiving can elevate entire societies, reducing poverty and creating a more equitable world.

While the solution of Diadidomi-focused prosperity is compelling, alternative approaches also merit consideration. Social entrepreneurship, for instance, combines the acumen of business with the mission of social change, creating enterprises where profit and purpose are intertwined. Another is the implementation of universal basic income, a concept that seeks to provide a financial safety net for all, ensuring that the basic needs of every individual are met.

As we navigate through the intricacies of this dialogue, a question emerges: Is it within our power to reshape the landscape of prosperity? Can we redefine success not merely by the accumulation of wealth but by the legacy we leave for the betterment of society?

Imagine a community where each individual's success is seen as a collective victory, where the fruits of one's labor not only nourish their family but also sow seeds of opportunity for others. Here, prosperity with a purpose becomes a tangible reality, a testament to the transformative power of Diadidomi.

So, let us embark upon this journey with resolute steps, understanding that prosperity, when tied to a higher purpose, becomes a force that can uplift, heal, and unite. It is a call to action, a challenge to embrace a prosperity that transcends mere wealth and becomes a beacon of hope for a world in dire need of vision and shared success.

Stewardship and Responsibility

In the interplay of light and shadow, where the opulence of some overshadows the scarcity of many, the principles of Diadidomi beckon us toward a higher calling—a stewardship of resources that demands not only wise management but also a heartfelt responsibility. The goal, an evergreen garden where the fruits of wealth nourish the soil of society, is within reach. This is a journey of transformation, a path that begins with the individual and ripples outward to the collective human experience.

The necessary prerequisites for this journey are not only material but also deeply rooted in the human spirit. One must possess an understanding of the Diadidomi framework, a willingness to embrace change, and a keen sense of empathy for the plights of others. With these in hand, the path to responsible stewardship can be navigated with clarity and purpose.

Imagine a tapestry woven from countless threads, each representing a step in the stewardship process. This broad overview captures the essence of the journey: the awakening of consciousness, the assessment of resources, the planning of distribution, the act of giving, the reflection on impact, and the continuous cycle of improvement. Each thread is integral, each step a milestone on the road to a more equitable world.

As we delve into the finer details, consider the awakening of consciousness as the dawn that dispels the darkness of ignorance. Here, the individual becomes acutely aware of their wealth, not as a static hoard but as a dynamic tool for change. The assessment of resources follows, a meticulous inventory of one's financial, intellectual, and social capital. This leads to the planning of distribution, the strategic blueprint that outlines how resources can be allocated to achieve the greatest good.

The act of giving, then, is not a mere transaction but a transformational moment—a redistribution of wealth that echoes the ancient rhythms of Diadidomi. With each gift, the giver steps further into the role of steward, planting seeds of opportunity that will grow into forests of prosperity for others.

Amidst these detailed steps, a compendium of tips and warnings emerges. Be vigilant, for the path of stewardship is fraught with the temptation to revert to old ways. Embrace transparency in your actions, for secrecy breeds distrust. Above all, remember that the measure of your success is not the magnitude of your wealth but the depth of your impact.

To validate successful completion, one must look beyond the ledger. True validation is found in the thriving communities, the empowered individuals, and the eradication of want. It is a legacy written not in the cold ink of bank statements but in the warm smiles of those whose lives have been touched.

But what of the troubles that may arise? When the well of generosity runs dry, or the recipients of your stewardship mismanage their newfound resources, it is not the end of the journey but an invitation to reassess and readjust. In the spirit of Diadidomi, every challenge is an opportunity for growth, a chance to refine your approach and deepen your commitment to the cause.

And so, amid the cacophony of a world that shouts for more, let us whisper an invitation to a different kind of wealth. Let us ask ourselves, "How can I cultivate a garden of abundance for all?" Through vivid imagery, let us paint a world where wealth is not the towering tree that blocks the sun, but the forest that shelters all life beneath its canopy.

Let our sentences dance with the cadence of conviction, our language simple yet profound. Let us punctuate our prose with the power of one-line truths that echo in the silence they create. And through quotations from those who have walked this path before us, let us find the wisdom to forge our own way.

In the stewardship of our resources, we are all artists, painting the future with the brushstrokes of our decisions. And in showing, not telling, we can inspire others to join in the masterpiece that is responsible Diadidomi—a legacy of wealth that is measured not in the gold it accumulates but in the lives it enriches.

The True Riches

In a world where the clamor of coins and the rustle of banknotes often dictate the tempo of life, where does one find the true riches? This question, like a seed planted in the fertile ground of the mind, sprouts a concept both ancient and revolutionary: Diadidomi.

To discern the essence of true riches, one must first grasp Diadidomi. A term of Greek origin, Diadidomi means "to give through" or "to distribute." It speaks to the act of passing something to another, of sharing with intention and purpose. It is an act of generosity that transcends mere transaction, embodying a spirit of mutual benefit and community enrichment.

True riches, within this framework, are not quantified by the weight of one's wallet but rather by the depth of one's impact on the world. They are found in the intangible assets of character—compassion, wisdom, and integrity. These are the keystones of a prosperous life, one that values relationships over revenue and purpose over profit.

Historically, the concept of wealth has evolved, yet the thread of Diadidomi weaves through time, visible in the philanthropic endeavors of ancient patrons, the charitable institutions of medieval times, and the social enterprises of the modern era. It reminds us that the act of giving has always been at the core of societal advancement.

To contextualize true riches within a broader framework, one must consider the ecosystem of humanity. Just as a tree's strength lies not only in its visible trunk but also in its unseen roots and the soil that nourishes it, so too does a person's true wealth lie in the unseen—their values, actions, and the community that grows around them.

Consider the entrepreneur who builds a business not solely for profit but to create jobs and solve societal problems. Or the teacher whose lessons ignite a passion for learning in students, and whose future achievements become part of the teacher's legacy. These are but two examples among count-less others where the principles of Diadidomi manifest in the real world.

However, common misconceptions about wealth persist. It is often believed that to be truly rich, one must accumulate and hoard resources. This is a myopic view that ignores the transformative power of sharing and the reciprocal nature of giving. True riches flourish when they are circulated and invested in the well-being of others.

Engage with this thought for a moment: If you were to count the treasures of your life, would you tally banknotes or the times you've made a difference in someone's life?

Too often we adorn ourselves with adverbs and adjectives, striving to decorate our lives with evidence of material success. But the true measure of wealth lies in the verbs and nouns—the actions taken and the lives touched.

A single line can sometimes capture the essence of truth more effectively than a lengthy explanation: Wealth is not what you have, but what you give.

Our language must remain as clear as a mountain stream, accessible and refreshing to all who seek its wisdom. For in the simplicity of words, the profound truth of Diadidomi can be shared widely, touching hearts and changing minds.

Let us then listen to the cadence of our choices, the rhythm of our giving, and the melody of a life rich with purpose. Where quotes and dialogues enliven the text, let us draw from the well of collective wisdom, "We make a living by what we get, but we make a life by what we give," as Winston Churchill once said.

And so, we must show the world what true riches look like, not merely tell of their existence. Through a canvas of anecdotes and descriptive vignettes, we illustrate the beauty of a life lived in the service of others—a life where Diadidomi is the brush, and true riches are the masterpiece it reveals.

In conclusion, the true riches in a world governed by the principles of Diadidomi are those that contribute to the collective prosperity of humanity. They are riches that echo through generations, not in the echo of jingling coins, but in the reverberating acts of kindness, wisdom imparted, and communities uplifted. They are the riches that, once shared, return to us in forms far more precious than gold.

Testimonies of Abundance

Dawn had not yet broken when Maria set out from her modest home, a small basket of fresh bread in hand, moving toward the center of the village. The cobblestone streets whispered tales beneath her feet, each a testament to the lives of those who tread before her. The air, crisp and expectant, seemed to hold its breath as if awaiting the day's unfolding story.

Maria, whose wrinkles etched a map of generous smiles and countless worries, was a pillar in this tight-knit community. Her small bakery, a labor of love passed down from her grandmother, was more than a place of commerce; it was a sanctuary where the scent of warm dough was the salve for a weary soul.

As the sun crept over the horizon, bathing the village in

amber light, Maria approached the town square. There, a young man sat huddled beside the fountain, his eyes echoing the hollow of uncertainty. His name was Alex, a soul adrift on the tides of misfortune, his dreams capsized by harsh economic reality.

Maria, guided by an unseen compass, approached Alex. She handed him a loaf, her eyes meeting his with the kindest of inquiries, "What troubles you?" Her voice was the melody of concern, a harmony of the heart that resonated within him.

Alex shared his tale, how he had aspired to be an artist, to capture the world's beauty on canvas, but the weight of poverty had shackled his hands, and his spirit had wilted. Maria listened, her heart a vessel for his sorrow, and in that moment, an invisible thread wove a connection between them.

The unexpected journey began with that simple act of sharing, a testament to the transformative power of Diadidomi. Maria offered Alex a job at the bakery, not out of pity, but from a recognition of his potential. In return, Alex would paint a mural on the bakery's wall, a beacon of hope and beauty for all who passed.

As days turned to weeks, the mural blossomed under Alex's brush, a vivid tapestry of village life. His once-dormant talent now enlivened the community, stirring a wellspring of inspiration. Maria watched, her heart full, as patrons of the bakery lingered longer, drawn by the art that now framed their conversations.

The story of Maria and Alex, while unique, was a microcosm of the universal truth that Diadidomi seeks to illuminate. The act of giving, of opening oneself to another's potential, enriches not only the recipient but the giver as well. The abundance they experienced was not merely economic but spiritual, a wealth that rippled outward, touching lives beyond their own.

Have you, dear reader, ever considered the breadth of your impact when you extend a hand in kindness? The concept of Diadidomi challenges us to look beyond the superficiality of material accumulation and to understand that true abundance comes from the heart's capacity to give.

The wisdom you stand to gain from these pages is the realization that each act of giving is a seed planted, one that can grow into a tree under whose shade others may find shelter. Maria's gesture toward Alex was a single drop in an ocean, yet it created ripples that reshaped their world.

I, Kirk Anthony, have witnessed these principles in action. From the moment I heard the divine voice as a child, to my scholastic achievements and military service, I have seen how giving creates a tapestry of interwoven lives, richer and more vibrant than any solitary thread.

As we venture further into this narrative, let us ponder this:

when was the last time you experienced the joy of giving, of seeing your actions elevate another's life?

The stories that follow are not mere tales but testaments to the power of Diadidomi. They are the voices of those who have discovered that true wealth is not counted in currency but in the currency of love, wisdom, and community.

In a one-line truth, let this resonate within you: To give is to receive wealth beyond measure.

I invite you to turn the page not just with your hand but with your heart open, ready to receive the abundance that comes from the simple, profound act of Diadidomi. Let us journey together through testimonies that whisper to our souls the secrets of a truly abundant life.

8

———

THE DIADIDOMI VISION FOR THE FUTURE

A New Economic Paradigm

Step into a realm where the impossible becomes the blueprint for reality, where the chains of fiscal inequality shatter, and where the seeds of sustainable prosperity are sown for all. This is not a utopian fantasy; this is the promise of "DIADIDOMI," a revolutionary concept that is set to redefine the very essence of our world economy.

Imagine a system where the principles of giving and receiving are not just acts of individual kindness but are woven into the fabric of our global economic policies and practices. This is the world you are about to enter—a world where the ancient Greek term "diadidomi," meaning to give over or to share, becomes the key to unlocking a future of unparalleled equity and sustainability.

As Kirk Anthony, I have been graced with the gift of foresight and the ability to distill complex concepts into actionable truths. From the divine whispers I heard as a child to the accolades of academia and the honor of military service, each step of my journey has led me to this pivotal moment. Here, at the intersection of spirituality and econometrics, I extend an invitation to you: to join me in constructing a world where economic transactions are imbued with the spirit of generosity and reciprocity.

Why should you believe in the transformative power of Diadidomi? Because it is more than a theory—it is a practice that has been tested and refined through rigorous analysis and real-world application. It is a methodology anchored in a deep understanding of economic systems, human psychology, and spiritual truths. It creates a synergy that not only suggests but insists that a better world is within our reach.

But I hear your doubts. How can such an idealistic vision work in the complex, cutthroat reality of our global economy? How can altruism possibly align with the relentless pursuit of profit? It is natural to be skeptical of change, especially one that challenges the very foundations of our economic beliefs. Yet, history teaches us that it is often the most radical ideas that reshape our societies for the better.

Let us, together, paint the picture of this new world. Envision local communities flourishing as businesses adopt Diadidomi practices, circulating resources and creating opportunities. Picture multinational corporations redefining success, measuring their worth not solely in profit margins but in their contributions to societal well-being. Imagine governments enacting policies that incentivize sustainable practices and equitable wealth distribution.

This journey is not a solitary one. It requires the collective will and determination of individuals, businesses, and nations. It demands a reevaluation of what we value and a steadfast commitment to the well-being of our planet and its inhabitants. As you turn each page, you will discover the framework for implementing Diadidomi at every level, from personal finance to international trade.

The value of this book lies not just in its vision but in its practicality. It offers a life-changing potential that extends beyond mere economic reform; it proposes a new way of living, of being in the world. The principles of Diadidomi, when applied, can lead to personal growth, stronger communities, and a healthier planet.

Why settle for the status quo when a brighter future is within our grasp? Why cling to outdated models that perpetuate disparity and destruction? The time for change is now, and it begins with embracing the Diadidomi principles. This book is not just a reading experience—it is an invitation to become an architect of a new economic reality.

Do you dare to envision a world where wealth is not hoarded but shared, where growth is not measured by consumption but by contribution, where the economy is not a battleground but a fertile ground for collaboration? This is the world DIADIDOMI promises, and it starts with you.

With every chapter, expect to be challenged and inspired. Anticipate moments of revelation and opportunities for transformation. This is not just a book; it is a manifesto for a new economic era. As you embark on this journey, remember that the power of change lies within you. Your actions, no matter how small, can ripple through the economy, creating waves of positive change.

Are you ready to be part of this economic renaissance? Are you prepared to adopt the principles that will reshape our world for generations to come? If your answer is yes, then welcome to "A New Economic Paradigm." Together, let us build a legacy of prosperity, equity, and sustainability—a testament to the enduring power of Diadidomi.

Spiritual Renaissance

In the dim corridors of history, humanity has often stood at the crossroads of transformation. One such transformative epoch unfurled as the Renaissance period dawned upon Europe, heralding an age where the human spirit soared to new heights in art, science, and philosophy. It was a time when the collective consciousness awakened, and individuals became acutely aware of their potential within the grand tapestry of existence. Yet, as we traverse the corridors of the present, an even more profound awakening is on the horizon —a Spiritual Renaissance.

Travel back in time to the Age of Enlightenment, where reason and individualism began to challenge the dogmas of the past. Philosophers like Kant and Rousseau debated the nature of humanity and our place in the universe. These conversations planted seeds that would eventually burgeon into the diverse spiritual landscape we navigate today.

The Historical Milestones that paved the way for our current spiritual inquiry are numerous. The Great Awakenings that swept through various societies shook the foundations of traditional religious structures, giving rise to a multitude of denominations and interpretations. Fast forward to the 20th century, when the New Age movement began to synthesize Eastern and Western thought, introducing practices such as meditation and mindfulness to the Western world.

From Past to Present, we see the threads of these movements weaving through our global fabric. Today, the world grapples with the existential threats of climate change, social inequality, and a pandemic that has upended lives globally. These crises have prompted an inward turn, a questioning of the values that underpin our societies. In a world teetering on the brink of various precipices, individuals seek solace and meaning, reaching for something transcendent to anchor their lives.

Why History Matters Now becomes evident when we consider our yearning for connection and purpose in a seemingly fragmented world. Understanding our spiritual lineage allows us to recognize patterns and possibilities within the chaos. It is within this context that "DIADIDOMI" emerges as a beacon of hope, a principle that has the power to drive a global spiritual awakening akin to the Renaissance of old.

Segue to the Story of our Contemporary Exploration, where we delve into the heart of this awakening. As we stand amidst the cacophony of modern life, "DIADIDOMI" whispers of a different way—a path that leads away from the relentless pursuit of material wealth and toward a reality where spiritual fulfillment is interlaced with every aspect of our being.

Dare we envision a world where economies serve not only the body but also the soul? Where the success of a society is measured by the well-being and spiritual growth of its people? It is a profound pivot, one that requires not just a change in policy but a transformation of the heart.

With every passing day, the signs of a spiritual renaissance grow stronger. People from all walks of life are beginning to question the narratives that have long governed their existence. They seek a deeper connection, not just with one another but with the very essence of life itself. Within this quest, there is a growing recognition that the act of giving—of sharing our resources, our time, and our love—is perhaps the most potent catalyst for personal and collective evolution.

What if, within the concept of "DIADIDOMI," lies the blueprint for an enlightened society? What if, by embracing the art of giving, we unlock a higher consciousness that propels us toward a future that is both spiritually rich and materially prosperous?

Imagine a community where "DIADIDOMI" is not merely a practice but a way of life. Visualize the streets humming with the energy of cooperation, the air thrumming with a palpable sense of unity. Here, businesses thrive not through cutthroat competition but by nurturing the seeds of generosity. Governments operate not on the currency of power but on the wealth of shared values.

But how, you may ask, can such a vision be realized in the tangible world? It begins with the individual—a single soul igniting the flame of change within. It spreads through conversation, through the sharing of ideas and ideals. It is sustained by the collective will to create a world that reflects our highest aspirations.

As we navigate the tumultuous waters of our time, let us anchor ourselves to the principles of "DIADIDOMI." Let us be the architects of a new spiritual epoch—a renaissance that will be remembered not only for the grandeur of its vision but for the depth of its humanity.

Are you ready to be a harbinger of this spiritual renaissance? Will you embrace "DIADIDOMI" and allow it to transform your life and the world around you? The journey is arduous, the path less trodden, but the destination—a world awakened to its spiritual potential—is a vision worth striving for. Welcome to "Spiritual Renaissance," the next chapter in our collective saga, where the spirit of giving becomes the cornerstone of a new civilization.

Global Policies for a Diadidomi World

In the intricate web of our global ecosystem, every thread of policy and practice weaves into the fabric of society's progress. The current issue at hand, which reverberates through the corridors of power and the streets of the common man alike, is the economic disparity that has taken root in the very soil of our civilizations. This disparity, if left unchecked, threatens to erode the foundations of stability and peace across nations.

The crux of this challenge lies in the unequal distribution of wealth and resources. A stark contrast has emerged between the opulent lives of a fortunate few and the dire struggles of the many. This divide is not just a matter of financial inequity; it is a multifaceted dilemma that includes access to education, health care, and opportunities for personal and community growth. It is a problem that feeds into a cycle of poverty and despair, stunting the potential of generations and breeding societal unrest.

If this imbalance persists, the consequences are not hard to envision. A world riddled with strife, where the chasm between the 'haves' and 'have-nots' leads to social upheaval, political instability, and a breeding ground for extremism. A world where the environment is sacrificed on the altar of unchecked consumption, and where the spirit of community is supplanted by a survivalist mentality that pits neighbor against neighbor.

But what if there's a solution—a method that not only addresses the economic symptoms but also heals the societal fabric torn by disparity? This is where the spirit of Diadidomi comes into play, proposing an economic framework that is predicated on the art of giving and the equitable distribution of wealth.

The solution takes shape in a series of bold, yet practical, policies. Let us begin with the concept of a Global Minimum Tax, a policy designed to prevent large corporations and the ultra-wealthy from exploiting tax havens. By setting a floor for tax rates, countries can ensure that those with the greatest economic power contribute their fair share to the societies from which they benefit.

Next, consider the implementation of Universal Basic Assets—a portfolio that includes access to education, housing, and healthcare as fundamental rights, not commodities to be bartered. By guaranteeing a baseline of security, we enable individuals to rise above the survival mode and engage in the economy as innovators and entrepreneurs.

To breathe life into these policies, a multi-tiered approach is necessary. It begins at the international level, with agreements forged between nations to uphold these economic standards. It then filters down to national governments, which must enact legislation and create incentives for businesses and individuals to align with Diadidomi principles.

Evidence of the efficacy of such solutions can be drawn from smaller-scale experiments around the world. For instance, countries that have implemented forms of minimum tax or basic income have seen not only a reduction in poverty but also a spur in economic activity, as the additional resources are channeled back into the market.

Certainly, there are alternative solutions, such as laissez-faire economics or protectionist policies, which have their proponents. However, these often exacerbate the very issues they seek to solve. The Diadidomi approach, on the other hand, offers a synthesis that nurtures both individual initiative and collective well-being.

Can you imagine a world where corporations view tax not as a burden but as a contribution to the flourishing of the communities that host them? Picture a society where every individual, regardless of birth or circumstance, has access to the tools needed to carve out a fulfilling life.

This vision is not mere utopia; it is a blueprint for a world that values the spirit over the ledger, where giving becomes the axis upon which the economy spins. It requires a metamorphosis of mindset, from the myopic pursuit of personal gain to the acknowledgment that our fates are intertwined.

The rhythm of such change will not be swift or simple. It will ebb and flow, with setbacks and victories in equal measure. Yet, the cadence of progress, once set in motion, is difficult to arrest. It is propelled by the shared resolve to craft a world that mirrors our noblest aspirations.

Let us then consider: What role will you play in this grand design? Will you be a bystander, or will you lend your voice, your effort, and your resources to the cause? The Diadidomi world is not a mere dream; it is a possibility that awaits the touch of our collective hands. Together, let us forge a future that stands as a testament to the power of giving—a legacy that will illuminate the annals of history for generations to come.

Diadidomi in Daily Life

As we ponder the grand tapestry of societal transformation through the ethos of Diadidomi, it is essential to recognize that the fabric of change is woven not only in the halls of governance but also in the quiet corners of our daily lives. The journey toward a world enriched by the spirit of giving begins within the hearts of individuals—within your own heart—and manifests in the choices you make every day.

Establish the Goal:

Your mission, should you choose to embrace it, is to embed the principle of Diadidomi into the very marrow of your personal and professional existence. The objective? To live a life that actively contributes to the well-being of others promotes fairness, and builds communities where prosperity is shared.

List the Necessary Materials or Prerequisites:

To embark on this transformative path, you'll need a few essential tools:

- An open heart, willing to give without immediate expectation of return.

- A discerning mind, to seek out opportunities where your contributions can have the greatest impact.

- The courage to act against the grain of self-interest when the common good is at stake.

- A community of like-minded individuals, because collective efforts amplify the power of Diadidomi.

Begin with a Broad Overview:

The journey of Diadidomi in daily life unfolds in several stages:

1. Cultivation of a giving mindset

2. Identification of giving opportunities in personal life

3. Application of Diadidomi in the workplace

4. Creation and nurturing of a community network

5. Reflection and adjustment of giving practices

Dive into Detailed Steps:

1. Cultivation of a Giving Mindset:

Transforming your outlook begins with simple daily affirmations that align your thoughts with generosity. Each morning, ask yourself, "How can I contribute today?" Let this question be the compass that guides your actions from dawn to dusk.

2. Identification of Giving Opportunities in Personal Life:

Look for moments in your routine where you can offer time, resources, or skills to benefit others. It could be as straightforward as mentoring a neighbor's child or as committed as volunteering for a local charity.

3. Application of Diadidomi in the Workplace:

Enrich your professional environment by initiating projects that serve broader societal needs. Advocate for fair trade practices, support diversity and inclusion, or propose corporate giving programs that match employee donations.

4. Creation and Nurturing of a Community Network:

Connect with others who share your vision. Build a network where resources, ideas, and support flow freely.

This could mean starting a community garden, organizing a local Diadidomi day, or setting up a platform for skill-sharing.

5. Reflection and Adjustment of Giving Practices:

Periodically reflect on the impact of your actions. Gather feedback, assess the outcomes, and refine your approach. Continual improvement ensures that your efforts remain effective and meaningful.

Offer Tips and Warnings:

- Embrace patience; change is a slow process, and your efforts may not yield immediate results.

- Beware of burnout. Giving is enriching, but you must also take care to replenish your own reserves.

- Avoid the savior complex; your role is to empower, not to impose your own vision upon others.

Testing or Validation:

Measure the success of your Diadidomi practices by the positive changes you observe in your surroundings. Are relationships stronger? Is your community more cohesive? Do you find fulfillment in your contributions?

Troubleshooting (optional):

If you encounter resistance or apathy, do not despair. Revisit your approach, seek counsel from your network, and remember that every act of giving, no matter how small, plants a seed for the future.

Vivid Imagery:

Visualize a morning where every greeting holds the promise of kindness, and every handshake is an unspoken vow to uplift. Picture a workplace where the buzz of collaboration hums with the undercurrent of shared purpose.

Direct Questions:

Have you noticed the subtle shift in your interactions when you approach them with the intent to give? Can you sense the strengthening bonds within your circle of influence?

One-Line Paragraphs:

A single act of generosity can ripple through the fabric of society.

Use Simple Language:

It's not about grand gestures, but the everyday willingness to lend a hand.

Emphasize Rhythm and Cadence:

Like the steady beat of a drum, each act of giving sets the rhythm for another.

Quotations or Dialogues:

As a mentor once said, "In giving, we receive; in sharing, we find abundance."

Show, Don't Tell:

Don't just tell your children about Diadidomi—involve them in preparing meals for those in need, and watch their empathy blossom.

Diadidomi in daily life is not a lofty ideal; it's a path walked in humble shoes, one step at a time. It is an invitation to each of us to step forward and play our part in the dance of giving and receiving that keeps the human spirit thriving. Will you take that step today?

The Legacy of Generosity

The tapestry of human history is rich with the threads of generosity, woven through the ages as a testament to our capacity for altruism. This narrative is not just a chronicle of past deeds but a beacon for the future, illuminating the path toward a society where the legacy of generosity endures and thrives.

Tracing the origins of generosity, we embark on a journey back to the earliest human societies. Throughout history, acts of giving have been recorded, from the sharing of resources among hunter-gatherers to the establishment of communal granaries in ancient civilizations. These initial steps laid the groundwork for a culture of mutual aid and support that transcended the mere struggle for survival.

As empires rose and fell, the concept of generosity evolved, often becoming institutionalized through religious tithes, alms for the poor, and the endowment of public works. Imagine the construction of aqueducts, libraries, and universities, all underpinned by the philanthropic spirit of their benefactors. Each stone placed was not just a physical contribution but a symbolic gesture of goodwill for generations to come.

Visual aids, like frescoes of communal feasts in ancient Pompeii or etchings of Victorian philanthropists, serve as poignant reminders of how generosity has been depicted and celebrated across different epochs. These images capture the essence of sharing and caring that has always been at the heart of human interaction.

The tapestry becomes more intricate as we examine the cultural and regional variations in the evolution of generosity. In some cultures, giving is a silent, personal act, whereas, in others, it is a public celebration. Festivals like India's Daan Utsav or the potlatch ceremonies of the Indigenous peoples of the Pacific Northwest embody the diverse expressions of this timeless virtue.

The modern interpretations of generosity are no less varied. Today, we see an ever-expanding array of forms—from microloans that empower entrepreneurs in developing nations to sophisticated digital platforms that facilitate global giving. The spirit of Diadidomi now lives on not only in individual acts of kindness but also in the collective action of social movements and non-profit organizations.

Yet, the journey of generosity is not without its challenges and controversies. Debates rage over the efficacy of aid, the ethics of philanthropy, and the impact of charity on systemic change. The turning points in this narrative often arise when generosity intersects with justice—prompting us to question whether our giving addresses the root causes of inequality or merely its symptoms.

Have you ever considered the immense power of a society driven by generosity? Can you envision a world where every individual is both a benefactor and a beneficiary of this virtuous cycle?

A single line can carry a weight of truth: Generosity begets generosity.

Let's speak plainly—the essence of Diadidomi isn't found in grand pronouncements but in the quiet resolve to make a difference, one life at a time.

Through the ebb and flow of sentences, let us feel the rhythm of countless hands joining together to uplift the weary and heal the broken.

"In every smile shared, in every burden eased," a sage once mused, "we see the true measure of our humanity."

Show the beauty of generosity not through lofty words but through the simple tale of a child who, with wide-eyed wonder, plants a tree, knowing they may never enjoy its shade.

The Legacy of Generosity is not a static relic of the past; it is a living, breathing force that propels us toward a future where the best of what we are is preserved and passed down through the ages. It is a call to action—a challenge to each of us to weave our own thread into the fabric of history, crafting a tapestry that will warm the souls of generations yet to come.

www.ingramcontent.com/pod-product-compliance
Lightning Source LLC
Chambersburg PA
CBHW071333150726
47997CB00002B/702